IN A PIG'S VALISE

book and lyrics by
Eric Overmyer
music by
August Darnell

BROADWAY PLAY PUBLISHING INC
New York
www.broadwayplaypublishing.com
info@broadwayplaypublishing.com

IN A PIG'S VALISE
© Copyright 1989 by Eric Overmyer

I S B N: 978-0-88145-657-8

First printing: January 2016

Book design: Marie Donovan
Page make-up: Adobe Indesign
Typeface: Palatino

IN A PIG'S VALISE was first presented as part of the Playwrights 86 series at Center Stage (Stan Wojewodski, Artistic Director; Peter Culman, Managing Director) in Baltimore.

IN A PIG'S VALISE was then produced in New York at the Second Stage Theatre, Robyn Goodman and Carole Rothman, Artistic Directors, with a new score by August Darnell. The first performance was on 11 January 1989, with the following cast and creative contributors:

JAMES TAXI..Nathan Lane
DOLORES CON LECHE .... Ada Maris
ZOOT ALORS .... Jonathan Freeman
ROOT CHOYCE.. Thom Sesma
THE BOP OP ....Reg E Cathey
BLIND SAX .... Charlie LaGond
SHRIMP BUCKET ....Michael McCormick
GUT BUCKET.. Jonathan Freeman
MUSTANG SALLY ....Lauren Tom
DIZZY MISS LIZZY.. Dian Sorel

Bass ....Carol Colman
Guitar..Eugene Grey
Saxophone .... Charlie Lagond
Keyboard ....Peter Schott
Drums ....David Span

Direction & choreography .... Graciela Daniele
Set design .... Bob Shaw
Lighting design ....Peggy Eisenhauer
Costume design...Jeanne Button
Musical direction ....Peter Schott
Sound design.................................... Gary & Timmy Harris

CHARACTERS

JAMES TAXI, *a private eye*
DOLORES CON LECHE, *a thrush*

denizens of the Heartbreak Hotel:
ZOOT ALORS *
ROOT CHOYCE
THE BOP OP,
BLIND SAX

the notorious Bucket Brothers:
SHRIMP BUCKET,
GUT BUCKET

THE BALKANETTES, *back-up singers:*
MUSTANG SALLY
DIZZY MISS LIZZY

* The actor who plays ZOOT *plays* GUT BUCKET *(in a fat suit)*

The action takes place in and around The Heartbreak Hotel, at the corner of Neon and Lonely.

AUTHOR'S NOTE

IN A PIG'S VALISE is a genre comedy. The genre
being simultaneously sent-up and celebrated is the
hard-boiled detective novel, invented by Raymond
Chandler. The true subjects of this comedy are genre
style and language, genre myth and image.

"Don't kid me. My nerves are frayed," I said. "Who's the junky?"

"Come along, Alfred," the big man said to his companion. "And stop acting girlish."

"In a pig's valise," Alfred told him.

The big man turned to me placidly. "Why do all these punks keep saying that?"

Raymond Chandler, *The Little Sister*

for Mark Herrier & Becky Gonzalez

ACT ONE

(Lots of fog)

(A streetlight. A couple of neon signs. Pale pink 'n blue neon fluid script)

(Heartbreak Hotel. Bar)

(Music: Opening Titles, a smoky instrumental, sax solo, something slow sultry sweet sexy sad and blue.)

(The music starts and swells. The fog drifts and swirls. The sign flashes:)

(Ba Ba Ba Ba Ba Ba Ba)

(A car approaches. Headlights. Fades away. Brakes screech on rain slick streets.)

(A match is struck. With panache)

(A man steps out of the fog. You know what he looks like: slouch hat, thread-bare suit, five o'clock shadow, no tie. Under his suit jacket he's wearing a pajama top instead of a shirt.)

(And he's very very short.)

(His voice is cool and tired.)

TAXI: Chaka chaka chaka cha. *(Pause)* Listen, baby.

(He sings NEON HEART, a hot and cool ballad about the life.)

NEON HEART

It was a foggy night
I heard a sax on the soundtrack
Somewhere a neon light
Flashed me right back to you
I walk the lonely streets
Cruisin' clues on bar stools
My heart's got a private beat
So cool it's neon blue

You know it's lonely out there
Streets are rainy and bare
And the whisky is starting to pour
I know what you're longing for
Goin' to the Neon Heart
You know that's where the records start
You know that's where they keep on keeping the score

I ease the Chevy slow
Ridin' around with the top down
I pay the tab and go
And I drive home alone

Money slick changes hands
Honeyed licks from the trombones
She makes you understand
Going to the Neon Zone

(Sax Solo)

You know the neon's so fine
All the saxophones shine
And the dancers are dreaming in bars
Tell me that it's time to part
Goin' to the Neon Heart
You know that's where the records start
You know that's where you'll find the mysteries are

You say "No Vacancy"
But I'm gonna make you love me

It'll be yours to take
Turn me off watch me fade
Watch my Neon Heart break...

Sweet finish.

(He sizes up the audience)

TAXI: As long as we're here. Let's smash the bubbly.

(He lights up. The smoke from the cigarette curls up in the blue streetlights, and his cool pose is the essence of a classic Forties album cover.)

TAXI: It was two-fifty-two in the fretful A M. I'd been ensconced in the back of my Chevy Bel-Air, dreaming I was a fresh-pressed Sinatra seventy-eight, with classic Forties water-color cover art. Pastels. I could've spun that particular platter all night long, until the grooves screamed for mercy. Instead, I found myself shivering in my shoes—scratch that—my gumshoes, on one of the worst corners in this quadrant of Western Civ. There were a lot of corners reserved for the criminally insane in this behind-the-eight-ball burg, but this one was special. Neon and Lonely.

(He drags on his cigarette.)

TAXI: Neon and Lonely. The co-ordinates of desire. Sax solos. Neon longing. Convertibles. Stolen convertibles.

(An acid belch)

TAXI: I'd come in from the valley. Forty-suck-your-heart-out miles of fast food and singed ozone. Avec shot brakes and smoldering upholstery. I was risking a loitering rap in front of a beanbag hotel. The kind of dive where checkout time sometimes comes when you least expect it. Loitering with intent: to meet some mysterioso-ette. Here. In the shadow of The Heartbreak.

(The neon Heartbreak Hotel sign pops on. He regards the classic pink and blue sign sourly.)

TAXI: Fleabag, beanbag, paperbag, scumbag, douchebag, bodybag hotel. Bagatelle. The Heartburn. This place is a case.

(He sneezes.)

TAXI: It was another damp one. The latest in a series. It seemed like a lifetime ago that I'd gotten her call. The call that had me sucking up bronchial smog and the kiss-me-deadly night air on the corner of Neon and Lonely with red eyes and flat fleet.

(Beat)

TAXI: Feet.

(Beat)

TAXI: The air was like liquid paper. Whoo. My chronic hypothermia was coming on like a bit of purple haze. Cold cojones, pal. I was shaking like a maracas player on the Feast Day of Saint Zenophobe of the Green Card. I played a round of pocket pool and kept hanging in. The fog continued to ladle itself on. Like pea soup in a Merchant Marine mess hall. Like interest on an easy-payment credit plan. Like suffering similies in exhausted sub-genres of pop-fic and modern lit. You couldn't hack through it with an M-16. Not that I had one. On me.

(Beat. Drags)

TAXI: All in all, a sweet, sweet set-up for a sap like me.

(Beat. Drags)

TAXI: But I couldn't leave. They'd towed my car. The kiss-me-Wednesday night air was putting a chill on my bones like jelly on a gefilte fish. I took a moment to strike a match on my eyebrow and set fire to another coffin nail.

(He strikes a match on his eyebrow, lights a second cigarette, smokes both.)

TAXI: One more thing. When I face front and talk to you this way—this way! This is the Voice Over voice. The Big V O. When you earn your P I license, they issue you your own V O. Don't let it slow you down. Just pretend that my lips don't move and you can hear my voice surple out over the PA all muffled and crunkly. I'm supposed to be thinking, see.

(He snuffs one cigarette.)

TAXI: But what I'm really doing is passing on vital exposition as we make an incomplete transition from pulp to performance. In other words, if I didn't tell you, you'd never know.

(Beat)

TAXI: It's gotta be how it's gotta be. We're all prisoners of genre.

(Music)

TAXI: Warning! If your own personal V O sounds pre-recorded, odds on it's a head cold. Maybe sinus.

(Beat)

TAXI: The name is Taxi. James Taxi. Mother calls me— when she calls me—Nancy James.

(He snuffs second coffin nail.)

TAXI: The voice at the other end of the line had had an Hispanic accent that was sweet as sucre and resonated like dollar signs in my ears. I won't perjure myself and tell you that the prospect of meeting that voice in person wasn't better than a poke in the eye with a sharp forty-five. I needed the job.

(The phone rings. He answers it. Flashback music)

TAXI: Give it to me straight.

*(The Flashback Music segues into KISS ME DEADLY sung
by* DELORES *who emerges from a phone booth.)*

DELORES: I'm looking for someone to help me out
No cop no doctor just a private eye
Oh, listen to me Taxi hear me out
I'm looking for a stand up guy

I need help give me a hand
I need help I'm in a helluva jam
If you heard my tale you wouldn't believe your ears
You could not conceive it in a million years
A conspiracy and such a deadly plot
These people are out to get me whether I'm ready or
   not
They want to, they want to, they want to they want
to…

Kiss me deadly
Make me quiver and quake
Kiss me deadly
Keep me wide awake
Kiss me deadly, deadly, deadly
They want to mesmerize me

Are you the man to crack this case or not
There's plenty danger standing in the way
Are you tough enough to be my ace or what
Can you take a chance this is your lucky day

I need help give me a hand, I need help I'm in a
   helluva jam
It's muy crazy but come to my aid
I need a Philip Marlowe or a Sammy Spade
He'll have to, He'll have to, He'll have to, He'll have
   to…

Kiss me deadly
Make me shiver and shake
Kiss me deadly
Keep me wide awake

Kiss me Deadly, Deadly, Deadly
He'll have to mesmerize me…

(Music vamps.)

TAXI: Nice pair of lungs, Miss…

DELORES: Con Leche.

TAXI: Con Leche. What you've told me so far is close enough for *Cliff Notes*. Why don't we get together? You can fill in the fine print.

DELORES: Your place or mine?

TAXI: I only face off at center ice.

DELORES: Know the Heartbreak?

TAXI: Hotel for Mutants?

DELORES: That's the one. Meet me tonight at the Heartbrak, Mister Taxi. After Midnight. You can catch my act.

TAXI: I'm running a fever already.

DELORES: It's an eye-opener.

(Music up)

DELORES: If you could be the one to ease my grief
You'd trade your forty-four and your sore eye-teeth
For a chance to hang around with a girl like me
I got a voice like a frozen daiquiri

I need help give me a hand
I need help I'm in a helluva jam
If you take this caper
I'll make it worth your while
You may lose your life
But man you'll go with a smile
Aren't you tough enough
Aren't you tough enough
Aren't you tough enough to

Kiss me deadly
Make me quiver and quake
Kiss me deadly
Keep me wide awake
Kiss me deadly
Honey don't be shy
Kiss me deadly, be my personal private eye
Kiss me deadly, deadly, deadly
Come on and mesmerize me

(*Big finish*)

(DELORES *hangs up and disappears as lights and music dissolve.* TAXI *hangs up. He burps delicately.*)

TAXI: Those dissolves always make me motion sick. Whoever she was, she gave great phone. After I hung up the horn, I closed the office for the afternoon. I gave my faithful amanuensis, "Legs" Lichtenstein, the rest of the week off. She'd earned it. I hadn't paid her since fiscal '57. Legs. What a word jockey. But that's another story. I sauntered over to my local gin joint and tossed down a couple of muscles. For you rookies out there, a muscle is standard-issue detective drink: Kahlua and Maalox. Then I grabbed some shut-eye in the back of my Chevy. (*Beat*) Con Leche's voice haunted my dreams like guava jelly. Spread sweet and smooth. I was stuck on that voice. Like enamel on a molar. (*Sneezes*) If I come down with something. Neon and Lonely. The Heartbreak Hotel at Neon and Lonely. Love it.

(*A throbbing base line is heard.* TAXI *snuffs his cigarette and turns up his collar.*)

TAXI: Something funky this way comes.

(TAXI *slides into the shadows.* BLIND SAX, THE BOP OP, LIZZY, ROOT, SALLY, SHRIMP, *and* ZOOT *juke in.* ROOT *and* ZOOT *are carrying what looks to be a body, wrapped in plastic and frozen solid.*)

(The others are loaded down with funky tube gear and strange devices. All are heavily and obviously disguised. They do The Skulk, an instrumental dance number. The music is threatening and insidious, and the dancing slinky. Eventually they all skulk on into the Heartbreak.)

(ROOT and ZOOT have a little trouble negotiating the stiff through the doorway. One of the Heartbreakers—BOP— drops something.)

(TAXI steps out of the shadows and picks it up. It's a white, plump, three-fingered glove. The kind Disney characters wear.)

(The music seques into THREE-FINGERED GLOVE.)

THREE FINGERED GLOVE

TAXI: Is this a clue
Maybe not
A piece of the puzzle
A part of the plot
Or just an accident
A meaningless event
Not worth caring about

Well you can never tell
I guess I'll have to put it away
And save it for a rainy day
I'll just wait and see

Three-Fingered Glove
What is it good for
Three-Fingered Glove
Who's it belong to
I guess that he would have to be
A digital amputee
A sawmill worker or such
Not much to go on

Oh what the hell
You can never ever really tell

I guess I'll have to put it away
And save it for a rainy day
I'll just wait and see....

(DELORES *steps out of the shadows.*)

DELORES: Nice pair of—lungs, Mister Taxi.

(TAXI *hastily stuffs the three-fingered glove in his pocket.*)

TAXI: *(In the V O)* I had eggroll all over my kisser. An Hispanic hallucination was hovering in the vicinity like heat on a desert highway.

DELORES: You talking to me? And why the past tense, pal?

TAXI: It's a convention, sweetheart. You ain't supposed to hear, dig? It's for them. *(Indicates audience)* The Big V O. Keeps 'em au courant.

DELORES: Is a V O anything like an M O?

TAXI: *(Warily)* Maybe. Who wants to know? Let's just say I'm cogitating a capella.

DELORES: It's a free country.

TAXI: Don't kid yourself. Say, you got a Dramamine, sister? I got a case of dissolve sickness. I feel like a side o' slaw strewn across a soggy paper plate.

DELORES: These hard-boiled similies get pretty thin. As thin as the skin on a cup of hot cocoa.

TAXI: As thin as the crust on an East Coast pizza pie.

DELORES: Neon and Lonely. Great spot for a rendezvous.

TAXI: This corner is seedier than a strawberry.

DELORES: And darker than a landlord's heart. Thanks for showing up, Mister Taxi.

TAXI: My pleasure, Miss Con Leche. Sleep is out of style this season. Let's get down to the storyline. What's the drumbeat, baby?

DELORES: I want you to locate something for me.

TAXI: Is it yours?

DELORES: Yeah.

TAXI: Sounds legal. Maybe we can do business. I have irresistible charm. Once you meet me, you never want to let me go.

DELORES: I find that difficult to swallow. Although I can believe the vice squad feels that way.

TAXI: They refer you?

DELORES: As a matter of fact, Mister Taxi, I picked you at random from the yellow pages. I was trying to call a cab.

TAXI: I've heard that one. If I had a thousand bucks for every time I've heard that one, I wouldn't be here now.

DELORES: I just assumed that all private dicks were alike—

DELORES & TAXI: (*In unison, more or less*) In the dark.

TAXI: Let's eighty-six the bright banter, shall we? And enough with the dick jokes. I hear enough dick jokes in the course of a day—

DELORES & TAXI: (*Unison, more or less*) To choke a horse.

TAXI: Okay, Con Leche. Lay it on me with a trowel. This missing something—stolen?

DELORES: Repeatedly.

TAXI: Once rabid, twice shy. Valuable?

DELORES: Priceless.

TAXI: Sure, sure, they all say that. I'm not your insurance company, lady.

DELORES: Uninsurable.

TAXI: No kidding. Description.

DELORES: Dreams.

TAXI: *(Sighs)* Could we be more specific, Miss Con Leche? What are we talking about here?

DELORES: Dreams. Someone is stealing my dreams.

TAXI: Dreams.

DELORES: Stolen. Lifted. Light-fingered. Long gone.

TAXI: Let's get literal, Miss Con Leche.

DELORES: *(Touching herself)* This is as literal as I get, Mister Taxi.

TAXI: Metaphor is for poets, kid. We hard-boiled guys go for palpable factology. We like simile. Like or as. Like a dream. As if in a dream. Except the kind that exist out there in the zeitgeist. You can put your meathooks on 'em.

DELORES: Zeitgeist?

TAXI: Like, my dream is a pair of center-court season tickets. My dream is a condo in the clouds. My dream is a garnet-colored jag with custom plates.

DELORES: You're slow, Taxi. I'm hablando-ing straight. Someone is stealing my dreams. My brain's being boosted. Look.

(Flashback Music)

DELORES: It all began a month ago. I answered an ad —

TAXI: *(Detecting ferociously)* What ad? Where?

DELORES: Cool your jets. This ad for folk singers. Ethnic folk dancers. That's my profession. They were hiring ethnic folk dancers down at the Heartbreak Hotel.

TAXI: Flashback me back, baby, and don't skip the slow parts. Sure you don't have a Dramamine?

DELORES: Watch my tracks, hard guy.

(*Music. The front of the Heartbreak opens up.*)

(*Seedy. Pathetic palms and pink flamingos.*)

TAXI: Wow. Spiff City. Turn down the ambience.

DELORES: It grows on you.

TAXI: I'll bet.

DELORES: The ad said ask for a Mister Bucket. So I did.

(DELORES *walks in.* TAXI *remains outside, watching the flashback.* ZOOT *is at the desk.* BLIND SAX, BOP, *and* ROOT *and enter.* DELORES *hesitates in the doorway.*)

ROOT: Yo, Bop.

BOP: Yo, Root.

ROOT: Yo, Zoot.

ZOOT: Yo, Root.

ROOT: Yo, Sax.

(BLIND SAX *plays a riff. Phone rings.* BOP *and* ROOT *pull gats, and aim at phone, as* ZOOT *answers.*)

ZOOT: Heartbreak Hotel—no vacancies.

(*He slams down phone. Offstage gunshots, screams, shattering glass.*)

ZOOT: Maybe I spoke too soon.

TAXI: (*Waves* DELORES *in*) Don't stop now. It's just getting interesting.

(DELORES *walks in.*)

ZOOT: Yez? Mai ah elp yew? Dew yew rechoir un rheum?

DELORES: Pardon you?

ZOOT: Dew yew ave un reservasion?

DELORES: *No habla* whatever language that is.

BOP: Reservations, ya need 'em?

DELORES: No, thanks, I got plenty already. I'm looking for Mister Bucket.

ZOOT: Wheech Monsieur Boockette? Oui ave deux Monsieurs Boockettes.

DELORES: I want to speak to the Mister Bucket who's looking for ethnic folk dancers.

BOP: She wants the Fat Man, Zoot. Give him a ring.

ZOOT: Honkey dorey.

(He rings. BOP cruises DELORES.)

BOP: What kinda ethnic dancing you do, Miss—

ZOOT: Allo, Monsieur Shreemp ou Monsieur Le Fat Man?

DELORES: Con Leche. Call me Dolores.

ZOOT: Zere ees une dancair ethnique en zuh lowbie, Monsieur Shreemp.

BOP: Okay, Dolores, call me Bop. Everybody does.

ZOOT: *Oui. Oui. Bon temps roulez, Monsieur.*

DELORES: Okay, Bop. I do all kinds.

BOP: No wheezing.

DELORES: You name it.

BOP: Slavic?

DELORES: Slavic, Serbian, South Philly —

ZOOT: Monsieur Boockette ees on iz whey.

DELORES: Que?

BOP: Hang ten, the boss is on the lam.

DELORES: The ad didn't say I'd need simultaneous translation.

(SHRIMP enters. Very bad taste: polyester and velvet.)

SHRIMP: May I help you?

DELORES: I hope so. I'm here about the ethnic dancing ad.

SHRIMP: *(Sizing her up)* Yes, yes, you look the part. Of course, I don't hire the dancers, I just run the audition.

DELORES: *(Alarmed)* Mister Bucket?

SHRIMP: I'm Mister Shrimp Bucket. My brother, Dr Gut Bucket —

(Ominous underscoring from BLIND SAX *whenever* GUT's *name is mentioned.)*

*(*TAXI, *watching the flashback, pricks up his ears.)*

TAXI: Hmm. Ominous underscoring.

SHRIMP: —has final say-so on the ethnics. I do the local talent. Yo-yo artists. Geeks. Talking dogs. My brother, Doctor Gut—

(Ominous underscoring)

SHRIMP: —is tied up in the Ice Bucket at the moment. If you'd care to wait, Miss—

DELORES: Con Leche.

SHRIMP: Con Leche. Zoot, ring Root. Been dancing long?

DELORES: Yeah.

SHRIMP: Good. Good. That's swell.

ZOOT: *(Into phone)* Root? Zoot. Toot Sweet.

DELORES: *(Overly casual)* You feature ethnic dancing? Or is this a new thing?

SHRIMP: Ethnic dancing? Are you kidding? We're famous for it. The Clam Room: Tops in Ethnic Dancing. The best Ethnic Dancing in Town. Wow. We just lost our lead ethnic dancer. She'd been with us for quite some time.

DELORES: Why'd she leave? Didn't she like it here?

SHRIMP: She loved it. But she had to get out of the business.

DELORES: Have I heard of her?

SHRIMP: You ask a lot of questions. For a dancer. Mitzi Montenegro. Know her?

DELORES: No.

SHRIMP: I find that hard to believe, Miss Con Leche. Small world, ethnic dancing. In fact, you look a little bit like her, the more I think about it. Kind of a smudgy carbon copy, you might say. Let me intro the leftover staff. That's Zoot Alors. He's—the night man.

DELORES: We met.

ZOOT: Yew bet. Enchante. Pairhops Ah could interest yew in un course of stoody a L'Ecole Maurice Chevalier?

SHRIMP: God I love the way you say that. This is the Bop Op. The Bop Op is wearing a brown pin-stripe suit, a brown button-down shirt from Brooks Brothers, brown socks, brown tie, brown Florsheim shoes, and chocolate brown Bill Blass boxer shorts. He's a very conservative dresser, but that's okay, we love him. And don't mess with him. He's a brown belt.

BOP: Hotel Security. How ya doin'?

(ROOT *enters.*)

SHRIMP: This is Root Choyce, Third World piano bar piano player and part-time ponce. Root tickles the ivories in the Clam Room.

ROOT: I don't take requests, Mi Chinita.

(BLIND SAX *plays a riff.*)

SHRIMP: Oh, yeah. Out of sight, out of mind. This is Blind Sax.

DELORES: Nice to meet you, Mister Sax.

SHRIMP: We here at the Heartbreak like to say Blind Sax is "visually challenged".

DELORES: Okay, I can relate to that.

SHRIMP: I thought you could. Zoot, *cherchez les femmes*?

ZOOT: Les gals are in rehearsal, mon boss.

SHRIMP: A real duo, know what I mean? Well, now that you've met the suspects—

(Everyone laughs, "heh, heh".)

SHRIMP: —why don't you cool your heels? Your audition's tonight, right here in the lobby. Root, show Miss Con Leche to her room. My brother, Doctor Gut—

(Ominous underscoring)

SHRIMP: —will be with you shortly. I do hope it works out.

DELORES: So do I. Gracias so much, Mister Bucket.

SHRIMP: Don't mention it. In fact, don't ever mention it again. To anyone. Blind Sax, a little traveling music, please.

(ZOOT rings bell.)

ZOOT: Root.

ROOT: Zoot. Walk this way.

(BLIND SAX plays ominous underscoring as DELORES tries gamely to walk like ROOT as he wends his way to her room.)

DELORES: *(To TAXI)* That was easier said than done. This weird music was following me and I had a creepy feeling about the whole set-up.

TAXI: Could be the ominous underscoring. Hard-boiled tip number one: trust your underscoring. Did you know Mitzi Montenegro?

DELORES: *(Suspiciously evasive)* Why?

TAXI: I thought we might ring her bell. Check her pulse. Scan her polygraph.

DELORES: Never heard of her.

(DELORES *returns to the flashback and walks into a pool of light.* ROOT *hands her a key.*)

ROOT: Enjoy. *(He exits.)*

DELORES: This isn't the Holiday Inn, Toto.

(*She unwraps a hotel drinking glass and pours water into it from a pitcher: it foams madly.*)

DELORES: I'd have to be stupid to drink this.

(*She drinks. Lights and music as she swoons dead away. The room crackles and glows. She gets up, and dances in her sleep, talking to herself in Spanish, ending with "estarring Dolores Con Leche!" She stutter-dances back to the bed.*)

(DELORES *re-appears in a pin spot.*)

TAXI: You blacked out.

DELORES: Like there was no tomorrow. I knew the tap water in this town was muy malo agua, but oh man! When I came to, I staggered over to my audition. I had the strangest feeling I'd been dancing in my sleep. I was so tired my legs felt like Spandex.

(*She meets* SHRIMP *in the lobby.*)

SHRIMP: Miss Con Leche. Have a nice nap? You look so fresh.

DELORES: Is it safe to drink the water?

SHRIMP: Don't be ridiculous.

(MUSTANG SALLY *and* DIZZY MISS LIZZY *saunter in. They wear Balkan folk dancing outfits: full skirts, peasant blouses, beaded vests, braided hair, the works.*)

SHRIMP: Meet the Balkanettes.

SALLY: This is the last time I wear these duds, mollusc meat.

SHRIMP: Mustang Sally and Dizzy Miss Lizzy. Ladies, this is Miss Con Leche. She's here to audition for lead ethnic dancer.

SALLY: Shrimp, you etouffee. You promised to bag this ethnic dancing bull when Mitzi bit the bullet.

DELORES: Mitzi Montenegro?

SALLY: She a friend of yours, softball?

DELORES: Never heard of her.

SHRIMP: Clam down, Sal. Let's do this audition.

SALLY: Crustacean face.

SHRIMP: *(counting off)* Bupke, kasha, babushka, latke.

(THE BALKANETTES *do the BALKAN BOOGIE.* SHRIMP *"choreographs.")*

SHRIMP: All right, sell it, girls. 1 2 3 4 and down, up, down, up.

LIZZY: Down up, down up. Hey that's fresh!

SALLY: Bite mine.

(SHRIMP *joins them. They sing and dance.)*

SHRIMP & THE BALKANETTES:
Hey na a Bucharesti
O perestroika
O Stoli twist,
Hava nagila baba au rhum,
Pasha
Panama, panama, panama

(Big ethnic finish)

SHRIMP: HOY!

DELORES: You call that ethnic?

SHRIMP: I do.

LIZZY: He's the choreographer.

DELORES: Oh, it's good, but try this.

(DELORES *signals the* BAND. *The music changes to Liquid Latino. She does the sinuous steps of MANGO CULO.*)

(DELORES, *the* BAND, *and offstage voices sing MANGO CULO.*)

MANGO CULO

MANGO, MANGO CULO
MANGO, MANGO CULO

SHRIMP: *(Spoken)* Look at that cake action, girls!

MANGO, MANGO CULO MANGO, MANGO CULO

SHRIMP: *(Spoken)* Boogie me back to Bogota, baby!

MANGO, MANGO CULO MANGO, MANGO CULO

(Jungle noises)

OFFSTAGE VOICES: Shaka Zulu! Shaka Zulu!

MANGO, MANGO CULO MANGO, MANGO CULO

OH OH OH OOOO

(Flamboyant finish)

SHRIMP: Say, that was extra extra special. I'm impressed. What do you call that?

DELORES: Mango Culo.

SHRIMP: Catchy. I have to check with my brother, Doctor Gut—

(Ominous underscoring)

SHRIMP: —but I think we might have a relationship here.

DELORES: Oh, Mister Shrimp, gracias so much.

SHRIMP: Don't mention nada, I told you.

SALLY: Not too shabby.

LIZZY: I liked it.

SALLY: Hey, Mex.

DELORES: Que hey, Tex.

SALLY: You're good. Let me give you some unsolicited advice.

SHRIMP: Sally—

SALLY: Clam up, bivalve. I've seen your type before, Ceviche —

DELORES: Con Leche.

SALLY: At least once. Take it from me. Watch your steps.

LIZZY: See you at show time. It's going to be great working with you. Can't wait. Bye.

(They exit cake-walking.)

DELORES: What did she mean? Watch your steps?

SHRIMP: Isn't that something you dancers say to one another? Maybe she's afraid she can't cut the con carne.

DELORES: Oh no, she's good. Well, not that good.

(A phone rings. SHRIMP answers, listens a moment.)

SHRIMP: I couldn't agree more. *(Hangs up)* Miss Con Leche, you start tonight. My brother, Doctor Gut—

(Ominous underscoring)

SHRIMP: —was most impressed by your audition.

DELORES: But he didn't see it.

SHRIMP: My brother sees everything. He ate up your act with a spoon. Beautiful superb and I loved it. His exact words.

DELORES: Oh, that's bueno, Mister Bucket.

SHRIMP: Keep it under your fruit bowl, kid.

DELORES: I'm no little sister from Mar Vista, Mister Bucket. Carmen Miranda couldn't carry my maracas!

SHRIMP: I'm sure she couldn't. See you tonight in the Clam Room. And, Miss Con Leche—

DELORES: Yes, Mister Bucket?

SHRIMP: Try and get some rest. Heh heh.

(SHRIMP *cackles and exits. Lights and music dissolve.* DELORES *rejoins* TAXI.)

TAXI: *(In the V O)* It looked like a cut-and-blow-dried case of Mickey One, pure and simplex. I didn't put much stock in her yarm about sleep dancing and dream stealing. It was my job to soothe her fevered brow. Taxi, the human tranq.

DELORES: Don't do that. It makes me nervous.

TAXI: Sorry. I didn't make the mysterious Doctor's mug in the flashback lineup.

DELORES: I've been here for months, and I still haven't seen him. He's elusive. You gotta help me, Taxi. I need my dreams.

TAXI: Why? Why you? Why dreams?

DELORES: That's why I called you, Mister Taxi. That's your bag.

TAXI: That's my racket, and I'm gonna bag it. Lookee, Miss Con Leche, dreams aren't my limo. Hot merch, that's my feedbag. Your basic electronic tube gear that's taken a stroll in felony shoes. The spouse that's a louse, fun on the run. Dreams? I wouldn't know where to begin. I'd be standing there in my flat feet with this big black cartoon question mark balloon coming out of my mouth—and eggnog all over my mugshot.

DELORES: I'll give you a hand. How hard can it be?

TAXI: I told you, knock off the dick jokes.

DELORES: Really, you're too sensitive.

TAXI: It's my tragic flaw.

DELORES: Mister Taxi, someone is running a number on me. I wanna know who, and I wanna know why. Somebody's trying to cash my ticket. You think I'm *meshuga*, Mister Taxi?

TAXI: *Meshuga*? No. Exotic, but not meshuga. They say, Miss Con Leche, that if you don't dream you eventually book yourself a cruise on the Big Banana Boat. Somebody trying to flip your hotcakes. Now that's an old-fashioned celluloid motive I can get next to. Let's say somebody decides to interfere with your sleep. They convince you your dreams are being stolen. Try telling the cops somebody's stealing your sleep. You'd be a wasp-waist cinch for certification as a solid-gold paranoid.

DELORES: You're not such a slouch after all.

TAXI: It's a pretty out secnario, Miss Con Leche. Who'd buy a set- up like that?

DELORES: You would.

TAXI: You're right. I would. Look, before I dip my wick any further, let's get something straight between us. I get fifty clams a day. Plus plenty of sauce for expenses. Boil or steam, no fry. Doctor's orders. A hundred in front, before I even start breathing.

DELORES: No dinero. No habla B-movie lingo.

TAXI: Look, sis, you're cute and Hispanic as hell, and when I look up into the depths of those lucious dark eyes I get vertigo and Calico and Monaco and like that, but your good looks won't pay my bar bill.

(DELORES *bats her eyes. A lot*)

TAXI: I'm a sucker for a pretty face. Miss Con Leche, I didn't catch your moniker.

DELORES: Not Monica. Dolores.

TAXI: Dolores. Dolores Con Leche. Sorrows with milk.

DELORES: I didn't know you were quite the linguist, Mister Taxi.

TAXI: Hang around. I may surprise you. Since I'm on the payroll—may I call you Dolores?

DELORES: Not a chance.

TAXI: You're on. So, who wants to scramble your sweetbreads, sweetheart? Why such a screwy way of driving you batshit? I got a million questions, Miss Con Leche, and no answers. And in my book, that just doesn't add up. We're going to have to go back in.

DELORES: Walk this way. *(She starts off. What a walk)*

TAXI: *(In the V O)* But there was no way I could walk that way. She had a walk that made my circumlocutions look like straight talk. And a pair of gams that could raise gooseflesh on a tossed salad. And they went all the way up to the top of her legs. I didn't exactly put a down payment on her story—but her walk had me more than a little intrugued.

DELORES: Will you stop talking like that?

TAXI: Sorry. Bad habit. Too many years living alone.

(DELORES, mock sultry, puts her arms around TAXI.)

DELORES: Taxi, tell me. What's so private about a dick?

TAXI: It's not fair, you know. I'm an innocent victim of slang warp.

DELORES: I've been dying to know, why do they call them gumshoes, pal?

TAXI: Can the snappy patter with syrup, sister. I don't even understand it. Let's make waves. We'll look into this... Dream Snatch.

(Pause)

DELORES: Okay. Truce.

(As they start into the Heartbreak, TAXI *checks his gun.)*

TAXI: Rod. Roscoe. Gat. Heater.

*(*BLIND SAX, BOP, ROOT, *and* ZOOT *appear.* TAXI *sniffs.)*

TAXI: *(In the V O)* The Heartbreak was a definite sushi bar, crawling with once and future co-defendants.

(Hostile stares from the Heartbreakers)

BOP: House rules. No private moments. Talk to yourself again, buddy, you're history. You're a silent flick that's been sliced into guitar picks. Got me?

TAXI: Yeah. Yeah. I got ya.

DELORES: Chill out, you guys.

*(*SHRIMP *enters.)*

SHRIMP: Dolores. Looking forward to the show tonight, sweetheart. Those new steps are—what's the word? Crepuscular.

DELORES: Crepuscular?

SHRIMP: Why not? Who's your little friend?

DELORES: Mister Shrimp, this is James Taxi. He's here for the show. James Taxi, Shrimp Bucket.

SHRIMP: What's your racket, Mister Taxi?

TAXI: Talent scout. Really. How about you, Mister Bucket?

SHRIMP: This joint is chez moi.

TAXI: My condolences to the chef.

SHRIMP: You write your own stuff. I like that in a man. Let me intro the leftover staff. This is the Bop Op.

BOP: Hotel security. Got any valuables?

TAXI: Yeah.

BOP: Hand 'em over.

(BOP *gives* TAXI *a claim check, and pockets his wallet and watch.* LIZZY *and* SALLY *enter.)*

SHRIMP: A real duo, Mister Taxi. Mustang Sally and Dizzy Miss Lizzy.

LIZZY: Hi.

SALLY: Bite mine.

SHRIMP: Root Choyce palpitates the eighty-eights in the Clam Room.

ROOT: I don't take—

TAXI: Requests. But I got a request right now. Fast forward through the intro, pal. I caught 'em in the flashback.

SHRIMP: Miss Con Leche's been filling you in?

TAXI: In a manner of speaking.

SHRIMP: Good things I hope.

TAXI: Nothing but the best. The highlights of the low lifes.

SHRIMP: Well then, you already know that Professor Alors runs L'Ecole Maurice Chevalier.

ZOOT: Yew mai call moi Zoot. Pairhops I can interest yew in a course of stoody a L'Ecole Maurice Chevalier?

SHRIMP: God, I love the way you say that.

TAXI: You don't get French lessons at the better hotels. I find that comforting.

SHRIMP: We aim to be a full-service hotel. Professor Alors does not teach Fench, he teaches French accent.

ZOOT: Yew nevair know when an accent ague mai sev yewour life.

TAXI: *(In the V O)* Professor Alors' accent smelled like brie, and the whole joint gave off an over-ripe odor like a bistro on a bad day.

BOP: I warned you about that, fella. Don't make me have to get litigious with you.

ZOOT: Why yew talk lak zat? Lisson, yew should talk lak zees. Lak Moi. An yew can. Zo easy. Zhust enroll at L'Ecole Maurice Chevalier, ze worl will be your camembaert.

TAXI: *Tres bibliotheque*, pal, but I'll pass.

ZOOT: Zoot yourself.

SHRIMP: He also slings slang. You oughta take from him, Taxi. Be good for business.

TAXI: I don't follow you.

SHRIMP: You could use some work on your lingo noir, Mister Taxi.

TAXI: Lingo noir? I'm a talent scout, Mister Bucket, I told you.

SHRIMP: I know you did.

LIZZY & SALLY: A talent scout? A talent scout? Really?

TAXI: Everybody wants to be in show business.

SHRIMP: Talent scout, eh?

TAXI: Really. Trust me.

(TAXI *sings TALENT SCOUT.*)

TALENT SCOUT

TAXI: If you doff your duds or don a drag
I'll break a leg to catch your act
Got a kinky twist or a twisted gag
I'll do anything and that's a fact

Cause I'm a Talent Scout

LIZZY & SALLY: Talent Scout!

TAXI: Hear me out and I'll tell you what
It's all about
I'm a Talent Scout

LIZZY & SALLY: Talent Scout!

TAXI: Without a doubt I'm the one for sure
who's got the clout

If you do your gig in dry ice fog
You call my number I'll be there
I get the chills for a talking dog
You can trust my guts I'm on the square

Cause I'm a Talent Scout

LIZZY & SALLY: Talent Scout!

TAXI: Without a doubt, I'm the one for sure
Who's got the clout
I'm a Talent Scout

LIZZY & SALLY: Talent Scout!

TAXI: Let's do lunch! I got something we can talk about
Ohhh Ohhh
All the rappers and the tappers and the fakirs and the
breakers and the strippers with their zippers say Get a
load of this you Talent Scout
All the scribblers and the dribblers, all the smugglers
and the jugglers, all the wheelers and the dealers, all
the squealers and the stealers, all the coppers and the
boppers, all the talkers and the rockers Say take a look
at me you Talent Scout
Everybody wants to be in show business
I'm a Talent Scout

LIZZY & SALLY: Talent Scout

TAXI: Twist and shout, come on baby What we talk
about I'm a Talent Scout

LIZZY & SALLY: Talent Scout!

TAXI: Without a doubt, I'm the one for sure who's got the clout

ALL: I'm a TALENT SCOUT

(Big finish)

SHRIMP: I'm impressed, Mister Taxi. That was extra extra special. You oughta drop by the Clam Room on Amateur Night, take your chances.

TAXI: No thanks, Mister Bucket, I'm strictly a non-combatant. *(To* SALLY *and* LIZZY*)* Nice job, girls, really.

LIZZY: Stay for the show, Mister Taxi.

TAXI: Wouldn't miss it. What do you do? In the show, I mean.

SHRIMP: The Balkanettes sing back-up for Dolores.

SALLY: Temporarily. That is strictly a temporary arrangement.

SHRIMP: We'll talk about it later.

SALLY: You bet we will, prawn prick.

SHRIMP: Ladies, meet me upstairs in my office. If you'll excuse us, Mister Taxi.

*(*SHRIMP *and THE* HEARTBREAKERS *turn to go.)*

TAXI: Is Mitzi Montenegro still on the bill?

(They all wheel around and stare at TAXI.*)*

SHRIMP: You know Mitzi like I know Mitzi?

TAXI: It's my business to know, Mister Bucket. Every aficionado of ethnic dancing knows Mitzi Montenegro, the Balkan Bombshell.

SHRIMP: Miss Con Leche said she'd never heard of her. Which led me to blieve that Mitzi was—obscure.

TAXI: Oh. Well. Dancers. What do they know? Where's Mitzi boiling her bulgar these days? I'd like to catch her act.

SHRIMP: You're out of luck, Mister Taxi. The Balkan Blockbuster said so long to the ever-sweaty world of ethnic dancing some time ago. In fact, Mitzi's in— home appliances now. She's cool. Heh heh.

HEARTBREAKER: : Heh heh. *(They all exit.)*

TAXI: I guess Mitzi wasn't, you know—well-liked.

DELORES: Take it light, Tax. Cool the monologues.

TAXI: Don't tell me my business.

DELORES: I gotta go warm up.

TAXI: I'll take a quick snoop see. Glom some loose threads.

DELORES: Check out my room. Maybe you'll pick up something.

TAXI: That's what I'm afraid of. Just kidding. Don't hit me.

DELORES: Meet me in the Clam Room.

TAXI: Right.

(DELORES exits. TAXI alone.)

TAXI: *(In the V O)* Something Shrimp said had me sweating like a bad paint job. That crack about lingo noir. Were the flats of my feet showing? And Dolores. Who was she really? Femme fatale, fait accompli? The name meant sadness in Espanol. And I had a hunch this case was gonna bring me more than my share of grief. Why didn't she bag this gig? Something was keeping Con Leche tied to this clip joint. Was it Mitzi? What is Mitzi Montenegro to her, or she to Mitzi Montenegro?

(BOP has entered quietly behind TAXI.)

BOP: That is the question.

TAXI: *(Screams)* Hah! *(He turns around, hands in the air. Looks at BOP, looks at his own hands up, covers by pointing with both index fingers still above his head.)* What's your racket?

BOP: What's yours?

(BOP *frisks* TAXI, *who still has his hands in the air.* BOP *removes* TAXI's *rod.)*

BOP: Talent scout, huh?

TAXI: Show business is the toughest business there is, Mister Op.

BOP: Don't get cute. I'll just keep this for you. Until you check out.

TAXI: Where do I find Doctor Gut?

(Ominous underscoring. TAXI *starts.)*

TAXI: Geez, do you ever get used to the soundtrack shadowing you all over the set?

BOP: It's like traffic. I don't even hear it anymore.

(TAXI *ostentatiously picks his teeth with a dollar bill.)*

TAXI: What's your alias?

BOP: What's yours, big boy?

TAXI: I'm just another eggbeater, Mister Op—hanging around for some answers.

(TAXI *picks his teeth with a second bill.)*

BOP: You couldn't pry it out of me with a crowbar—

(TAXI *adds a third bill.)*

BOP: —that Doctor Gut—

(Ominous underscoring)

BOP: —is tied up in the Ice Bucket.

(TAXI *hands* BOP *the bills. He shakes them dry.)*

TAXI: How do I get to the Ice Bucket?

BOP: You don't. Off limits.

(TAXI pulls out a checkbook and writes him a check.)

BOP: Got two pieces of I D?

TAXI: My wallet's in your pocket.

BOP: And it's gonna stay there. Make an isosceles triangle and follow your nose. *(Looks at check)* Add a zero to this, I might get careless with my pass key.

(TAXI changes check. BOP tosses the key. TAXI catches it.)

BOP: Have it back in an hour.

TAXI: Beat it, thumbprint. I gotta talk to myself.

BOP: Whatever gets you off. *(He exits.)*

TAXI: *(In the V O)* Now that I had the keys to the kingdom, I decided to take the grand tour.

(Lights and music. TAXI in a spot)

TAXI: *(In the V O)* My first stop was the Ice Bucket. It didn't take a detective to find it. I just followed the dry ice to the front door.

(TAXI travels. Clouds of dry ice)

TAXI: *(In the V O)* The stairs were slicker than sea urchin roe.

(TAXI arrives at the Ice Bucket just as DELORES appears and knocks on door. SHRIMP answers. Dry ice and sax music seep out of the Ice Bucket.)

SHRIMP: Dolores. What a treat.

DELORES: *(Checking out dry ice)* Hey! *Muy hielo seco!*

SHRIMP: I thought dry ice *en Espanol* was *hielo carbonico.*

DELORES: Could be. Is Doctor Gut here?

(Ominous underscoring)

SHRIMP: No. But he left these for you.

(SHRIMP hands DELORES a vial.)

DELORES: Gracias so much.

SHRIMP: How's your insomnia?

DELORES: I'm syncopated. I think I've got anemia, too. I'm beat.

SHRIMP: You do look run-down. I'll have—

(Ominous underscoring starts. SHRIMP cuts it off.)

SHRIMP: You know who—prescribe some animal vitamins.

DELORES: Well. Okay.

SHRIMP: Trust me. They'll do you a world of good. Ciao.

DELORES: Later.

(SHRIMP ushers DELORES out. As she leaves, BOP joins SHRIMP.)

BOP: Dolores. What a dream, huh?

(He laughs uproariously.)

SHRIMP: Don't wear it out. Who's her friend?

BOP: Half-baked hawkshaw. Bargain-basement shamus. *(Takes out gun)* I relieved him of this antiquated armament.

SHRIMP: *(Gives BOP a look)* I knew it. I've got an instinct for these things. Why would our milky senorita bring a hawkshaw into the Heartbreak?

BOP: Maybe she's got wise. *(Smiles)* Mitzi got wise, too.

(BOP and SHRIMP share an unpleasant laugh.)

SHRIMP: Take care of him after the show. He mustn't muck up our meeting with the big noise from Nauru.

BOP: In my mind, he's already relegated to the dustbin of history.

SHRIMP: *(Gives him a look)* See how they're doing downstairs.

BOP: You're the boss.

SHRIMP: Yes. Yes, I am.

(Lights and music. SHRIMP fades. TAXI follows BOP.)

TAXI: *(In the V O)* I followed Bop to the laundry. Zoot was doing a quick starch and steam. He didn't seem too happy about it.

(BOP enters laundry. ZOOT holds up a three-fingered glove.)

ZOOT: *Cherchez* eets mate? Zere ees anozer one of zees. Ahve yew seen eet?

BOP: Uh-oh. Check his coat pockets?

ZOOT: Oui. Oui. Bon idear. Oh, eef Ah don't find zat gloove, zee boz weel be furryous.

BOP: More than furious. Livid, positively. Shrimp wants him to look his best for the Big Noise from Nauru. That means both gloves, babe.

ZOOT: Ah! I am un dead man! Monsieur Croque!

BOP: Relax. You don't want to hyperventilate down here in all this humidity. I'll take a look around outside.

ZOOT: Merci, merci. Yew are un lumberjacques of un prince.

BOP: For you, Frenchie.

(BOP blows him a kiss, and fades.)

ZOOT: Three-fingered glove. Where is the other?

(Lights and music. ZOOT exits.)

TAXI: *(In the V O)* Bop's passkey was solid gold. It was making things easy. Maybe too easy. My next port of call was a bug on the pay phone.

(Lights and music. TAXI puts a transistor in his ear, as ROOT appears in a pool of light talking on the phone.)

ROOT: *(On phone)* Hey, this is a sophisticated device. State of the art.

TAXI: *(In the V O)* Bingo.

ROOT: He's gonna get a look at their extra extra special stuff. They're gonna pull out the stops, kicks out the jams, and boogie their sneakers away for this hombre. Misterr Batsumashball, micro chip czar, the Mitsubishi of Nauru. Where is Nauru, anyway? I heard bird guano. The whole lousy island, nothing but bird guano. Bird guano is what I heard, chucko.

(Lights and music. ROOT out.)

TAXI: *(In the V O)* Suddenly there was more thickener in the plot than corn starch in a coffee shop cherry pie. The meter was still running on Bop's passkey. On my way to the Clam Room, I stopped off to chat up the Balkanettes.

(LIZZY and SALLY, in a backstage dressing room, wearing robes.)

SHRIMP: *(Over P A)* Five minutes, girls. Showtime.

SALLY: Invertebrate.

SHRIMP: *(Over P A)* Remember the new steps.

SALLY: They suck gazpacho, lobster breath.

SHRIMP: *(Over P A)* You ougta be nicer to me. Remember, ladies—Mitzi Montenegro.

SALLY: That etouffee'll rue the day he messed with Mustang Sally.

LIZZY: We better be careful. Remember what happened to Mitzi Montenegro.

SALLY: You just remember, two men on a raft and wreck 'em.

(TAXI appears.)

TAXI: Just what did happen to Mitzi Montenegro?

SALLY: Her career didn't work out—

LIZZY: The way she'd planned.

TAXI: What do you hear from Mitzi? Is she happy in home appliances?

SALLY: Why are you so interested in Mitzi, Mister Talent Scout? She was a lousy dancer.

TAXI: Mitzi was my client. I was her agent. That's a sacred relationship.

SALLY: We don't know where she is.

LIZZY: Honest. Hope you like the show, Mister Taxi.

TAXI: I have my doubts. Eastern European Ethnic Dancing. Unless the Bucket Balkanettes are in for a surprise.

SALLY: What do you mean?

TAXI: Two men on a raft and wreck 'em.

SALLY: Means scrambled eggs on toast.

LIZZY: Nuevo Huevo's gonna be the next big thing.

TAXI: Nuevo Huevo? New Egg?

SALLY: The Balkanettes are as passe as Raisinettes. From now on we're the Omlettes.

(They shuck their robes.)

SALLY: And Nuevo Huevo's our jam.

(They sing NUEVO HUEVO.)

NEUVO HUEVO

LIZZY & SALLY:
Two men on a raft and wreck 'em
Means scrambled eggs on toast
You can boil or poach or breck 'em
You can coddle fry or roast

Stretch one burn one whisky down
Nuevo Huevo's back in town

Two men on a raft and wreck 'em
Means scrambled eggs on toast
You can boil or poach or breck 'em
You can coddle fry or roast

Stretch one burn one whisky down
Nuevo Huevo's back in town

(LIZZY *scats through instrumental.*)

Stretch one burn one whisky down
Nuevo Huevo's back in town
Stretch one burn one whisky down
Nuevo Huevo's back in town

Oooh oooh back in town
Oooh oooh back in town
Oooh oooh back in town

(*Sexy finish*)

TAXI: I can definitely say I'm not altogether uninterested. We'll talk.

LIZZY & SALLY: (*Exit singing*) Oooh oooh back in town

TAXI: The questions were mounting up like a stack of unpaid utility bills, and I had to find the answers before somebody turned off the lights. I had a feeling this case wouldn't be brief...brief...this case...wouldn't be brief...

(*Rescued by the* BAND: *music.*)

TAXI: Showtime?

BAND: Showtime!

TAXI: (*In the V O*) That was my cue to cut to the chase.

(*The lights come up full on The Clam Room. A couple of tables. Chase lights.* BOP *is the maitre d'.*)

BOP: This way, Mister Taxi.

(BOP *seats* TAXI *at one of the onstage tables.* TAXI *is the only customer.*)

TAXI: Is it always this slow?

BOP: It's been better. What'll you have?

TAXI: Ramos fizz. Do I have to be this close? I'll get sequin burn on my retinas.

BOP: You're a talent scout, aren't ya?

TAXI: Right. Right.

(BOP *exits. Music! Chase lights! Spots!*)

(*The Clam Room*)

(*A gaudy sign.* SHRIMP *bounds on, mike in hand, big fanfare, his theme music: SHRIMP LOUIE.*)

(*The Band shouts the refrain from offstage:*)

SHRIMP LOUIE

SHRIMP: I'm a burnin burnin hunk of shrimp
Shrimp Louie
(*O Shrimp Louie*)
I'm a burnin burnin hunk of shrimp
Shrimp Louie
(*O Shrimp Louie*)
Don't fuss with the dressin'
Cause you know you ain't messin with Louie
(*Shrimp Louie to go*)
Shrimp Louie
(*Eat it every day*)
Shrimp Louie
(*Shrimp Louie to go*)
Shrimp Louie
(*Eat it every day*)
Shrimp Louie
(*Shrimp Louie to go*)
Shrimp Louie Louie Louie Louie...
YEAAHHH

(Big resolving chord from Band.)

SHRIMP: Thank you. Thank you. Thank you. So sweet
so sweet so really nice 'n neat. Hi. I'm your host,
Shrimp Bucket. Welcome to the always nectarious
Clam Room and our show, Crack of Dawn, I know
you're gonna just cream all over it— *(Waves to* TAXI*)*
Our special guest tonight, ladies and gentlemen, Mister
James Taxi, a big time talent scout. Thanks for joining
us, Jimmy, here in the ever-humid Clam Room. You're
gonna get an eyeful of local talent tonight, I guarantee
it. You slay me, Jimmy, right off the old drugstore
rack—saaaaaaaaaaaaaaaaaaaaaaaaay. *(Pointing to lights
out front)* Those mixed fruit gels are really something.
Talk about your saturated color! Wow! What is that?
Vacation pink! And lavender surprise! And over there
a hot rod cherry red! All the way from Vegas, these
guys do a super job, ladies and gentlemen, big hands!
Big hands! Aren't they beautiful superb and extra extra
special? Say, welcome to the ever-livid Clam Room!
The temperature's rising we're getting hot hot hot!
While we're waiting for our opening number here in
the ever-hepatatic Clam Room— *(Sings a la Johnny
Mathis)* Let me entertain you Let me conk your hair
(Toothy smile) That's just a teaser, folks. More of me
anon. And speaking of digits—direct from their record-
breaking engagement in the attic of the Heartbreaker,
where they've been going at it hammer and tong—
here to smash some of their very own platters, and
spread sunshine and broken petro-chemical plastic all
over the place—let's give a hot chowder Clam Room
wilkommen to—the Four Freshpersons! Doing their
latest—look out it's hot—Vegetable Medley! Vegetable
Medley! Ladies and gentlemen, the Four Freshpersons!

*(*BLIND SAX, BOP, ROOT, *and* ZOOT *in matching jackets, do
an all-purpose soul medley: wonderful harmonies, dramatic
shifts in rhythms, great synchronized dance steps.)*

@BODYCENT = VEGETABLE MEDLEY *(CAFFEINE)*

ROOT: Early in the morning and all through the night

QUARTET: Mainline mainline straight to my heart

ROOT: Caffeine caffeine Caffeine

QUARTET: Mainline mainline straight to my heart

ROOT: Put the spike to my heart and shoot it right in *(Whoosh)*
Put the spike to my brain and shoot it again *(Uhh)*
Give it to me baby make it hot and black

QUARTET: Mainline mainline

ROOT: Give it to me baby now don't hold back

QUARTET: Mainline mainline straight to my heart

ROOT: The pain the pain grab an available vein

QUARTET: To ease the pain you

ROOT: Grab an avaiable vein

QUARTET: Free refill free refill
Free refill free refill
Free refill free refill
Free free free
Free free

(Into)

THE ECHELON OF SCUM

BOP: I'm going up and down
On the carousel of crum
Floating to the top
Of the echelon of scum
I'm a bad bad guy
Don't need no alibi
I'm the cream of the crop

And I'm floating to the top
Of the echelon…

QUARTET: Ohhh echelon of scum

BOP: I'm a nasty man
And I know that's what I am
I got crime in my bones
I put slime on my scones
I'm the crown prince of quease
And I do just as I please
I'm the creme de la crum

QUARTET: I'm the sultan of scum

BOP: I'm the cream of the crop

QUARTET: And I'm floating to the top

BOP: Of the echelon…

QUARTET: Ohhhhhh echelon of scum

(The QUARTET whistles a chorus.)

(Into)

ETHNIC JOKES BROKE MY BABY'S HEART

TRIO: *(BLIND SAX, BOP and ROOT)* Didja hear the one?

ZOOT: That's what they say

TRIO: Didja hear the one

ZOOT: Every single day

TRIO: Those ethnic jokes

ZOOT: About my baby

TRIO: Those ethnic jokes

ZOOT: That drove her crazy

QUARTET:
Those ethnic jokes that broke my baby's heart

TAXI: I heard that one

ZOOT: It ain't funny

TAXI: I heard that one

ZOOT: You bet your money

TRIO: They'd tell those jokes

ZOOT: About her brother

TRIO: They'd tell those jokes

ZOOT: About her mother

QUARTET:
Those ethnic jokes that broke my baby's heart

BLIND SAX: *(Spoken)*
She's gone away now, I don't know where
To a place where they don't tell those kinds of jokes
To a better world…somewhere

BOP: *(Spoken)* I say…the melting pot ain't so hot!

ZOOT: Ethnic jokes about my baby
Ethnic jokes they drove her crazy
Ethnic jokes about my baby
Ethnic jokes they drove her crazy

QUARTET: Ethnic jokes they broke my baby's heart

(Into)

PUT YOUR LEGS ON MY SHOULDERS

QUARTET: Put your legs on my shoulders
Put my head in your lap
Wrap your kneecaps 'round my earlobes
And we'll do it just like that

Put your legs on my shoulders
Honey drive me 'round the bend
Let me dive right up on in you
Wake the neighbors up again
Hum Hum Hum Hum

Root & Zoot:
Honey your legs, ba-rooom, ba-rooom
Honey your legs, ba-rooom, ba-rooom

Zoot: Oh my darling when you kiss me
And we get so moist and slick
Just remember when you miss me
Let me give you one last lick

Quartet: Put your legs on my shoulders
Don't tell me I just ate
You know that I always told her
Grab my ears and aim me straight

Put your legs on my shoulders
Put my head in your lap
Wrap your kneecaps round my earlobes
And we'll do it just like that
Hum, Hum, Hum, Hum

Root & Zoot:
Honey your legs ba-rooom, ba-rooom
Honey your legs ba-rooom, ba-rooom

Zoot: O my darling when I meet you
And we go to bed in haste
Oh my darling when I eat you
I just long for one more taste

Quartet: Put your legs on my shoulders ooh, ooh, ooh
Put your legs on my shoulders ooh, ooh, ooh
Put your legs on my shoulders ooh, ooh, ooh
Put your legs on my shoulders ooh, ooh, ooh

OH OH OH OH OH OH OH OH AHHHHHHH
STOP!

(Big finish. The Four Freshpersons exit. The Band picks up the groove, as Shrimp *comes back on, clapping his hands in rhythm. The Four Freshpersons dance back on for an encore.)*

PUT YOUR LEGS ON MY SHOULDERS REPRISE

SHRIMP: All right everybody I want you to put your hands together and when I point to you I want to hear you say "Put Your Legs". Got it? "Put Your Legs" One two three

QUARTET: Put your legs on my shoulders
And I'll drive you round the bend
I know that you're feeling bolder
Wake the neighbors up again

SHRIMP: And should you be feeling colder
Put your legs

QUARTET: Put your legs

SHRIMP:	QUARTET:
Put your legs	Put your legs
Put your legs	Put your legs
Put your legs	Put your legs
Put your legs	Put your legs
Put your legs	Put your legs

QUARTET: On my shoulders YEAH!!

(The QUARTET *boogies off.)*

SHRIMP: The four freshpersons! The Four Freshpersons! Aren't they beautiful superb and extra extra special? They don't call 'em The Four Horsemen of the Acapella Lips for nothing. Heh heh heh. We'll continue with "Calamity in the Clam Room" in just a few days but first…I want to speak to you directly. *Mano a mano* as it were. That's the great thing about live theater. That communication… Can I have the house lights, please?

(House lights come up. SHRIMP *surveys audience.)*

SHRIMP: Great. That communication between us—and you. That living, breathing, okay mistakes can happen kind of communication. The theater is the last bastion of live entertainment. As you may not know—or even

believe—the price of a ticket doesn't begin to cover
costs. Not even close. There's what you see—lights,
costumes, sets, actors. The Band. And there's what
you don't see. Hidden costs. Limos, lunches, lingerie.
Ludes. Union kickbacks. Just kidding, fellas. Don't
turn off the lights. But seriously, there are hidden
expenses. And sometimes we just can't hide them
any longer. I don't think I have to tell you folks— *(To
audience member)* —try to work with the drug. With
it. *(Back to audience)* —I don't have to tell you about
inflation. A show like this one, expenses have just gone
through the roof over the last season. You know, if we
were to cover costs through ticket sales alone, we'd
have to sell each seat five times. Five times. And that
would be mighty uncomfortable. Think about it. Hey!
We're having some fun now! And now—accompanied
by the ever-lactating Balkanettes—the star of our
show—the filibrating thrush herself—the Hispanic
Hyperventilator—Dolores Con Leche.

(DELORES, *with* LIZZY *and* SALLY. *Splashy entrance,
gorgeous gowns, wigs. Motown heaven. They sing NEVER
JUDGE A THRILLER.)*

NEVER JUDGE A THRILLER

DELORES *with* LIZZY & SALLY:
Never judge a thriller by its cover NO
Never judge a thriller by its cover NO

I'm a thriller at large
A paperback broad
A killer babe
I need to be read out loud
Turn my pages sweetheart
And follow my plot
Don't skip a single chapter
Cause I'm hot hot hot

Never judge a thriller by its cover (Never, never, never)
Never judge a thriller by its cover (thriller)

I'm a chiller babe a drugstore dame
A femme fatale
That's my claim to fame
Don't you quit till we're done
Till we get to the end
Then we can start me all over again

(Refrain)

(During an instrumental break, BLIND SAX *wailing,*
DELORES *transforms herself into the classic image of a pulp
covergirl: strap down over one shoulder, cigarette, smoking
derringer. Thus transformed, she sings:* I'M A SPINE-
TINGLER, BABY—*but the lights suddenly go out, and the
sound grinds down, like a record player whose plug has just
been pulled. Then, just as suddenly, the lights come back on,
and music whirls back up to speed. In the blackout,* TAXI
*has gotten up and is standing in the middle of the stage. He
attempts to speak to* DELORES, *but she ignores him as the*
BALKANETTES *finish their set:)*

(NEVER JUDGE…cont.)

DELORES *with* LIZZY & SALLY:
I'm a spine tingler babe
A pulp coquette
Be a hard guy with me baby
You will not regret
Got a ruby forty-four
Got a cherry new Corvette
Better buy my cover baby
What you see is what you get

Never judge a thriller by its cover (Never judge a
    thriller)
Never judge a thriller by its cover (Thriller)
Never, never, never, never, never
Never, never nooo

Never, never, never, never, never
Never, never, noo
Never judge a thriller by its cover (NO)
Never judge a thriller by its cover (NO)
NO, NO, NO o o ohhhh

(Big finish. They exit.)

(SHRIMP bounds back on.)

SHRIMP: Dolores! Dolores! And the Balkanettes! They'll be back later with some authentic ethnic folk dancing! I guarantee it! Dolores and the Balkanettes! What a warbler! Now that's ornithology! And the dance steps! Don't you just love them? Better than synchronized swimming! They don't call them Balkanettes for nothing! Okay! Kung Fu fighting next! *(To TAXI)* Take your seat, fella. Hey! We're having some fun now! *(To audience member)* I spoke to you earlier about that. Work with the drug. The band does.

TAXI: I got a coupla plot points I'd like cleared up.

SHRIMP: You came in late, fella.

TAXI: That's where you're wrong. I've been over my neck in this from the very beginning.

SHRIMP: Come back tomorrow night. I'll flush the rust out of my pipes.

TAXI: I'll pass. I wanna know the whereabouts and general prognosis of Mitzi Montenegro.

SHRIMP: What's it to you?

TAXI: Mitzi was my client.

SHRIMP: Tell me another one, shamus.

(TAXI grabs SHRIMP by the lapels, and being so short lifts himself off the ground.)

TAXI: Why don't you buy my cover? What's your trick bag, sleazeball? Sing.

SHRIMP: Calm down, fella.

TAXI: And what was that little blackout about? Sounded like somebody pulled the plug.

SHRIMP: You wanna know a lot for the price of admission. Okay, I'll tell you. Yes, what you suspect is all too true. We lipsynch.

TAXI: Very nicely done.

SHRIMP: Thank you. Now you know our nasty little secret. How about you stop wrinkling the merchandise.

TAXI: How about you give me the straight dope on Mitzi Montenegro. If you wanna be around for your encore, pal.

SHRIMP: Since you put it that way, let me put it this way. And this way. And what about this way.

(*As* SHRIMP *puts it various ways,* BOP *brings in* TAXI's *drink. It's foaming madly.*)

TAXI: You're a literal kid of guy, Mister Bucket. Where's your brother, Doctor Gut?

(*Band plays ominous underscoring Las Vegas big Band style.*)

TAXI: I wanna have words with him.

SHRIMP: My brother is a busy man, Mister Taxi. He doesn't have time to play private eyes.

BOP: Your Ramos fizz, sir.

TAXI: Oh, no. I'm hip to this stuff.

SHRIMP: You make it hard on yourself, Mister Taxi.

(BOP *saps* TAXI. TAXI *crumples.*)

BOP: Later for you, lightweight.

SHRIMP: (*to* BOP) You young squid you. Let's blow this clam bar.

(SHRIMP LOUIE reprise. BOP, ROOT, *and* ZOOT*join*
SHRIMP.*)*

BOP, ROOT, SHRIMP, & ZOOT:
I'm a burnin burnin hunk of Shrimp (Shrimp Louie o
Shrimp Louie)
I'm a burnin burnin hunk of Shrimp (Shrimp Louie o
Shrimp Louie)
Don't fuss with the dressin
Cause you know you ain't messin with me
Of all the Louies which is the best (Crab Louie?)
No way (Saint Louie?)
Get real (Louie Louie?)
Even Louie Louie can't kick my bootie
Shrimp Louie
Shrimp Louie
Shrimp Louie to go
Shrimp Louie

Eat it every day

Shrimp Louie Louie Louie Louie Yeah!

(The HEARTBREAKERS *boogie on out, leaving the comatose*
TAXI *on stage.)*

(A blue spot on TAXI, *face down and unconscious. The spot
narrows to a pencil point, then extinguishes. When the house
lights come up for intermission, he is gone. But left behind is
a chalk outline of his body on the floor.)*

END OF ACT ONE

ACT TWO

(A bare stage. TAXI *saunters out, jacket over his shoulder, cool as can be, and sings PRISONER OF GENRE.)*

PRISONER OF GENRE

TAXI: I take my coffee black
With a slug of rye or three
I call my mother—"Mac"
And you can make all my moves—"B:"

I'm addicted to the style
And all my moves are noir
I'm a sucker for a smile
Across a crowded bar

I'm just a prisoner of genre, baby
I guess I've found my niche
I'm just a prisoner of genre, baby
A lonely captive of kitsch

I've surrendered to the slang

I make all my moves in raincoats
I got a gat in my pocket
If I thought I had a future
I'd run right out and hock it

I'm just a flat-out flake
I make out in smokey rooms
I'm dying for another take
And living for those zooms

I'm just a prisoner of genre, baby
I guess I've found my niche
I'm just a prisoner of genre, baby
A lonely captive of kitsch

J'adora my fedora

Tap City is my address
Where all the bulbs are bare
My haute cuisine is rice and beans
But I'll do it for the dare
(Spoken:) —plus expenses

I've been drugged and sapped
And slugged and slapped
Got neon on the brain
I risk my skin for just a fin
I'm a sucker for a dame

I'm just a prisoner of genre, baby
I'm so addicted to the style
So stamp me urgent and confidential
And slip me in your file
I'm just a prisoner of genre, baby
A prisoner, a prisoner—in style.

(Sweet finish. Lights dissolve to:)

(In front of the Heartbreak. TAXI, out like, well, like the classic sapped hard-boiled gumshoe.)

(A reggae bass beat)

(TAXI woozes to his feet.)

TAXI: *(In the V O)* I came to with a Mafiosa construction company slapping together a condo in my back brain. They were working overtime and pounding plenty o'nails. Two brothers, Guiseppe and Antoine. I clawed my way up through concentric spinning circles of trauma, dread, nausea, pain and primary motor dysfunction. *(Staggers)* I was dizzier than a dose of peroxide, and as feverish as a bottle of aspirin. My brain was pounding out a reggae back beat. Detective with eggcream all over his punim. C'mon, Taxi. Do something really tough—like get on your feet. You got a New York City driver's license. Prove you deserve it.

(TAXI *swoons.* DELORES, *entering, catches him.*)

DELORES: What's so macho about a New York City driver's license?

(DELORES *props* TAXI *back up.*)

TAXI: License to kill, sweetheart. License to maim.

DELORES: Natty Taxi. Someone caught you looking uptown instead of down.

TAXI: Just as I had your shrimp-faced boss squirming like aquarium bait. Whoo. I feel like a short chunk of beef jerky. Chewed. I'm fading faster than a forged check.

(DELORES *straightens him by the lapels.*)

DELORES: My dreams can't wait until tomorrow.

TAXI: Listen, as far as I'm concerned, your dreams can wait until Jimmy Hoffa shows up to claim his social security.

(*Reggae bass beat goes out. He starts off.*)

DELORES: Where are you going?

TAXI: Home. I've had it. I've had it being pushed around on no sleep, and I've had it being conned by my own client. There are easier and cleaner ways to make a buck, and I'm gonna go fine 'em. Right now.

DELORES: Taxi, you can't leave me. Okay, what do you want?

TAXI: I want you to level with me. Who is Mitzi Montenegro?

DELORES: Just another ethnic dancer.

TAXI: Sure, sure, They all say that. Say, I caught the show tonight. Boffo charisma, mucho melisma.

DELORES: What?

TAXI: You're a thrush. You may be an unreliable witness, but I dig the way you warble.

DELORES: Taxi, I didn't do the show tonight.

TAXI: Don't kid me. I was this far away from you. I may have trouble picking a perp out of a lineup—

DELORES: No way. I dropped one of Doctor Gut's brain bombers—

(Ominous underscoring)

DELORES: —to pep myself up, and I was out before you could say Tito Puente.

TAXI: Either you've got schizoid amnesia, or the Bucket Brothers have a first class female female-impersonator. Remember the blackout?

DELORES: How could I? I told you—

TAXI: Onstage. Somebody tripped the breaker. I got up and whispered to you. You didn't whisper back.

DELORES: Taxi, I'm telling you. It wasn't me.

TAXI: Mitzi Montenegro—what's she look like?

DELORES: How should I know?

TAXI: Come clean, Con Leche. She's as familiar to you as a hangnail. Who is she?

DELORES: My sister.

*(*TAXI *slaps* DELORES.*)*

DELORES: My sister!

*(*TAXI *slaps her again.*)*

DELORES: My sister!

*(*TAXI *slaps her again.*)*

DELORES: My sister! *(Slap)* My sister! *(Slap)* My sister!

TAXI: Not your daughter?

DELORES: My sister!

(DELORES *knocks* TAXI *down with a right hook. He picks himself up.)*

TAXI: I believe you. Don't hit me again. How long's she been gone?

DELORES: More than a month.

TAXI: Was Mitzi the type to take a powder and not leave a forwarding address?

DELORES: Mitzi knew something wasn't on the level. She was just about to go to the authorities when she disappeared.

TAXI: Cops?

DELORES: Health department. She's my kid sister, Taxi.

TAXI: Say no more. Where I come from, that counts for something. Don't worry, sweetheart. I'll find your dreams.

(DELORES *grabs* TAXI *and kisses him three times.)*

DELORES: *O, bueno! Mucho! Muchacho! Muchisimo!*

TAXI: *(In the V O)* Her lips were a palpable lip batido—

DELORES: Don't do that in front of me, Taxi. Na khazan.

TAXI: *Que tengo*, Con Leche. Whatever you do, don't nod off. Get a cup of joe. Trust me.

DELORES: I'll take my bombers.

TAXI: Don't you learn from experience? You're strung out like laundry. Fork 'em.

(DELORES *hands* TAXI *the vial* SHRIMP *gave her.)*

TAXI: Non-prescription speed only. Meet me in your room. I have to make a phone call.

DELORES: <MI>Bueno<D>! Let's locate Mitzi, Tax! Undulate! Undulate!

(She exits. He looks after her wistfully.)

TAXI: *(In the V O)* I would have given a lot to undulate with Con Leche right about then, but time was short and talk is cheap. I had a hunch if I could find Mitzi, I'd clear up this caper like linament on a charley horse. *(Beat)* Well, they can't all be gems. To reorient myself, I did a quick mental hit and run.

(LIZZY and SALLY in a spot)

SALLY: Her career didn't work out—

LIZZY: —the way she'd planned.

(SHRIMP in a spot)

SHRIMP: My brother left these for you, Miss Con Leche.

(DELORES in a spot)

DELORES: I'm not dreaming the dreams I once had.

(ROOT in a spot)

ROOT: This is a sophisticated device. State of the art.

(ZOOT in a spot. Holds up a three-fingered glove.)

ZOOT: Zere ees anozer one of zees. Have you zeen eet.

(SHRIMP in a spot)

SHRIMP: Mitzi's in home appliances now. She's cool. Hey, Tax— You're beautiful, baby. Don't ever shave.

(BOP in a spot)

BOP: *Comidas chinas y criollas! Mofungo!*

(All begin repeating their lines at once as the lights swim. A babble. TAXI cuts it off and everyone disappears.)

TAXI: *(In the V O)* Those mental hit and runs were rough to take on no sleep. And I wasn't any closer to finding out of Dolores' dreams were being stolen, and if they were, why. But I wasn't born yesterday. I've heard enough ominous underscoring in my time to know that at the bottom of it all was Dr Gut…

(Ominous underscoring)

TAXI: Bucket. *(Pats pocket)* What? *(Pulls out his gat)* Why had the Bop Op given me my gat back? It was time to recherchez the Heartbreak.

(Goes to phone booth. Dials.)

TAXI: Bucket. Shrimp. Residence. Same to you. *(Dials)* Bucket. Taxi. Taxi. I got something you want. Something you're looking for. Oh no? I wouldn't be too sure about that. Ask Professor Alors. Yeah, I'll hold.

(SHRIMP puts him on hold. Tinny muzak comes out of the phone. SHRIMP LOUIE.)

TAXI: Gee, I oughta get this for the office.

(Muzak stops. TAXI gets back on the line.)

TAXI: Surprised? What about this? Earlier tonight you smuggled a stiff into the Heartbreak. Isn't that the reverse of the house rules? My pleasure. You'll see me when you see me.

(TAXI hangs up. The Heartbreak opens up and TAXI walks in.)

TAXI: *(In the V O)* I took the shortest route to Con Leche's room.

(Music. He travels. Enters DELORES' room.)

(TAXI holds the pill vial up to the light. He reads the RX.)

TAXI: Take as needed for instant sleep. Catnap, one cap. Two caps: sleep soundly through sirens, heavy construction, marital discord, civil disorder, and decade's major cultural trends. For the Long Goodbye: scarf as many as fast as you can. Caution: do not ingest while vertical. *(In the V O)* It did not seem like such

a half-baked bad idea once I thought about it. I was
dragging bun. I needed forty winks like a Chinese
restaurant needs M S G. I would lie down on the job
and do a little field research at the same time. The place
to start putting the handcuffs on this sleep snatch was
Con Leche's pillow. *(Investigates bad wiring)* Kinky.
(Tries to open vial—can't) Detective-proof bottle. *(Gets
it open. Still standing, he shakes out a pill and pulls out a
pint.)*

TAXI: *(In the V O)* I crossed my palm with a logsawer,
and tossed down a slug. Then a distant bell rang in
the back of my cerebellum. Something about doctor's
orders. Something about verticaallllllllluuuuuuuuu —

*(His eyes roll back in his head and he's out in a dead faint.
The bed crackles and glows.)*

(Huge arc of blue light.)

(Honk and wail from BLIND SAX.*)*

(Weird greenish light up on TAXI, *who is standing looking
down at his sleeping self. Dream music, underscoring and
special effects.)*

TAXI: *(In the V O)* I was dreaming I had my own
weekly series. The James Taxi show. Starring James
Taxi. Beaucoup buckage. Endorsements. Fan mail.
In the series, I'm the divorced father of three teenage
private detectives. Two girls and a boy. It's a good
premise. Comedy-suspense. I was just sitting down in
my agent's office...

(Lights swim. Music swims.)

TAXI: *(In the V O)* —When suddenly there was a
blinding jagged flash—nothing but late night snow
on the small screen—purple and green afterburn on
the backs of my eyelids like I'd had a flashcube go off
in my face—cauterized cortex! My brain was being
processed like Spam!

(TAXI *dances back to the bed, jerking and twitching, a thousand volts of pure energy coursing through his body. He flops on the bed.*)

(*The lights stop swimming as* DELORES *enters.* TAXI *sits bolt upright.*)

TAXI: I'll take the pigs with me!

(DELORES *slaps* TAXI.)

TAXI: (*Shakes out cobwebs*) I gotta get a day job. What a night. What a head. Like a guacamole avocado.

DELORES: Taxi, what are you doing in my bed?

TAXI: Sacrificing my body to detective science. I downed one of these.

DELORES: My pepsters from Doctor Gut.

(*Ominous underscoring*)

TAXI: Yeah, these pepsters are first-class dozers, sweetcakes. Always read labels.

DELORES: Did you dance in your sleep?

TAXI: Like a linebacker. Jetes somnambules.

DELORES: *Que pasa,* Tax?

TAXI: When my head hit the pillow, the Buckets siphoned off my dream faster than a vice cop on the pad.

DELORES: Why you?

TAXI: Not me—you. They didn't expect anyone else to be using that futon.

DELORES: (*Outraged*) Taxi! What do you take me for—a nun? Just because you don't have any social life—

TAXI: Here's the scam—they've got Mitzi in the hotel somewhere, and she's doubling for you in the show. That wasn't you I saw out there tonight, it was your sister.

DELORES: My kid sister.

TAXI: Your kid sister. And believe me, where I come from, that counts for something.

DELORES: Why are they doing that to Mitzi?

TAXI: I don't know. But there's got to be major-league clammage, somewhere in this dream snatch. Hotel do well?

DELORES: Get real. This place doesn't do business on New Year's Eve.

TAXI: Go downstairs and stake out the lobby. If this jaspar from the Far East shows up, tip me. Jiggle the wiring.

DELORES: I don't care what they say about you, Tax. I think you're jake.

TAXI: James. And just what do they say about me?

DELORES: Oh hombre, por dios, no me hagas rerir!

(She exits.)

TAXI: (In the V O) I've always been a sucker for the enigmatic kind. I was overdue for a shrimp fry. I had something he wanted.

(Traveling music. TAXI arrives at the Ice Bucket anteroom. Dry ice seeps. A rattan fan chair. SHRIMP is practicing some moves with imaginary mike for SHRIMP.)

SHRIMP: (Acapella)
I'm a burnin' burnin' hunk of Shrimp
I'm a burnin' burnin' hunk of Shrimp
Don't fuss with the dressin'
Cause you know you ain't messin' with me—

TAXI: Brushing up your act, Mister Bucket?

SHRIMP: What's your professional opinion, Mister Taxi?

TAXI: Get out of the business.

SHRIMP: I think I sound pretty good without the band. Shrimp Louie—a ca paella. Heh heh.

TAXI: I get the driftwood. You're one bad egg.

SHRIMP: Your use of the idiom is dazzing. Of course, you show folk. Life in the demi-monde. Sit down, sit down. Take the Huey Newton Chair.

(SHRIMP *indicates the rattan fan chair.* TAXI *sits warily.*)

SHRIMP: Drink?

TAXI: Whiskey. Three fingers.

SHRIMP: *(Beat)* Three fingers, eh? Chaser?

TAXI: Neat. No attitude.

(ROOT *appears and hands* TAXI *a drink.*)

TAXI: Swift. I like that it's not foaming. What's the call brand?

ROOT: Heart of Darkness. The White Man's Bourbon. *(He exits.)*

TAXI: Why does he get all the good lines?

SHRIMP: Affirmative action.

TAXI: Affirmative action. The Huey Newton Chair. You make the Heartbreak Hotel sound like a museum, Mister Bucket.

SHRIMP: How perspicacious of you, Mister Taxi. Yes, the Huey Newton Chair is part of our American Icon collection. Huey endowed it.

TAXI: An endowed chair in a hotel?

SHRIMP: We're in a non-profit hotel. Huey was kind enough to leave us the chair.

TAXI: I'd like to take a gander at the rest of your collection.

SHRIMP: Not a chance. By appointment only. We're not a wax museum, Mister Taxi.

TAXI: Oh? I thought maybe you were. What was that package you had delivered in the wee wee hours? A new exhibit?

SHRIMP: A very old exhibit, Mister Taxi. We'd sent it out for a little refurburation. Now, Mister Taxi, I'm a busy guy. Belly up to the point.

TAXI: With pleasure. I decided to wink out in Con Leche's room. I popped a dubious dozer, and was out like a golfing doctor. While I was sawing my sheep, somebody lifted my dreams.

SHRIMP: Your—heh heh—dreams, Mister Taxi? What would anyone want with your dreams? Dreams are so personal. Like underwear. You never have to worry about having your underwear snatched from the laundromat. They're too personal. They wouldn't fit. (*Beat*) Dreams are the underwear of the mind, Mister Taxi. Why take somebody else's? No deposit, no return. That does double for sordid, soiled, soggy, no starch, sewer-snooper dreams like yours—the grubby shorts of a truly short subject.

TAXI: If you were in my line of work, Mister Bucket, you'd know there are plenty of creeps—right out there—who'll go for somebody else's boxers. But I'm not here to argue eschatology with you. I wasn't the intended. Nobody expected me to be on that futon. You were after Con Leche. You siphoned off my dreams because you thought they were hers. You're sucking up Con Leche's dreams like they were plankton. You've got her doped to the gills. Whatever you're using has a nasty side effect. It makes her dance in her sleep. She's no good in the act anymore, so you've got the supposedly missing Mitzi Montenegro doubling Dolores! You're an ethnic dancing junkie! Admit it! You're hooked!

SHRIMP: You're raving. How is such a thing possible?

TAXI: We may never know. But I intend to find out.

SHRIMP: If you'll excuse me, I've had enough of this bizarre conversation.

TAXI: Thanks for the gut bomb.

(Ominous underscoring from BLIND SAX*)*

TAXI: How do you do that?

SHRIMP: Aren't you forgetting something?

TAXI: Am I?

SHRIMP: You have something that belongs to me.

TAXI: Oh, you mean— *(He pulls the three-fingered glove out of his pocket.)* —a three-fingered glove?

*(*SHRIMP *lunges for it, but* TAXI *pulls his gat.* SHRIMP *puts his hands up. They sing a reprise of THREE-FINGERED GLOVE.)*

THREE-FINGERED GLOVE

TAXI: A three-fingered glove

SHRIMP: Where did you find it?

TAXI: A three-fingered glove

SHRIMP: What good can it do you

TAXI: A three-fingered glove
Why don't you tell me

SHRIMP: You're not a digital amputee...yet

TAXI: Are you threatening me?

SHRIMP: Just you wait and see

TAXI: Don't get tough with me

SHRIMP: It was my Grandpa's
An heirloom you see
He lost a pinkie
It means bupkes to me

TAXI: You can never ever really tell
I guess I'll have to put it away
And save it for a rainy day

SHRIMP & TAXI: You just wait and see!

(*Music out*)

TAXI: I'll do that.

SHRIMP: There's a reward.

TAXI: How much?

SHRIMP: Two Cs.

TAXI: Two Gs.

SHRIMP: Okay.

TAXI: A G is worth more than a C, right?

SHRIMP: Where I come from.

TAXI: How do I know this is really yours? It may belong to some digitally challenged person.

SHRIMP: I'll show you the mate.

TAXI: Sealed deal.

SHRIMP: Meet me in the laundry in ten. You drive a hard bargain, Mister Taxi. I'm not used to negotiating at gunpoint. The security at this hotel is terrible. My apologies.

TAXI: Don't count your dim sum before it's steamed, Mister Bucket.

SHRIMP: Don't press your duck, pal.

(*The lights blink conspicuously. Ominous underscoring. Lights restore to full and the underscoring phrase revs back up to speed and finishes.*)

TAXI: You oughta do something about your underscoring, it's death on wiring.

SHRIMP: *A bientot*, Mister Taxi. A pleasure doing business with you.

(SHRIMP *fades.*)

TAXI: *(In the V O)* I was in the vichyssoise no doubt about it. I had to make waves and fast. That power failure was a signal from Con Leche that the guest of honor was on his way.

(TAXI *travels.* DELORES *is waiting in the lobby.*)

TAXI: Where is he?

DELORES: *(Pointing)* Incoming at nine o'clock.

(MR BATSUMASHBALL *enters. He is played by* ROOT *in dark glasses, turban and sarong.*)

MR BATSUMASHBALL: Sorry, so sorry, I am looking for Mister and Mister Bucket—

DELORES: Oh yes, aren't you—

MR BATSUMASHBALL: Yes, I am Mister Batsumashball, from Nauru.

DELORES: Right. Mister Batsumashball, it was on the tip of my tongue.

(TAXI *slips up behind* MR BATSUMASHBALL *and sticks a gun in his ribs.*)

MR BATSUMASHBALL: I knew it! I knew it! I knew America was a dangerous country! Take my traveler's checks! Take my Rolex! But please don't take my cocoanuts!

TAXI: I'll settle for your sarong. Take his chapeau.

MR BATSUMASHBALL: Kinky American perverts.

(*The* BAND *plays strip music, as* TAXI *takes off his clothes and puts on* MR BATSUMASHBALL's *sarong. He puts on* MR BATSUMASHBALL's *dark glasses and sandals, as* DELORES *holds the gun on him.*)

TAXI: Take a brain bomber, pal.

(TAXI *stuffs one of the instant sleep capsules into* MR BATSUMASHBALL's *mouth—he's out on his feet instantly.*)

TAXI: Think of this as a hideous case of jet lag.

(*They stash him behind the palm.* DELORES *takes* MR BATSUMASHBALL's *turban and puts it on* TAXI.)

DELORES: You look good. Your turban is crooked. Chicks dig turbans.

TAXI: I'll remember that.

(DELORES *straightens it.* DELORES *and* TAXI *get tangled up.*)

TAXI: You got narrative structure, sister. You got plot points galore.

(DELORES *and* TAXI *are about to get into a heavy clinch when they hear voices.*)

ROOT: (*Offstage*) I don't care how blase you are, no one sleeps through the Big O.

(ROOT *and* BOP *enter.*)

BOP: Man, this scam is taking the scungilli outta my ramen.

(*Sees* DELORES *and* TAXI)

BOP: (*To* DELORES) I gotta question your taste in men. You the big noise from Nauru?

TAXI: I'm not Jackie O.

BOP: Jackie O got better shoulders, pal.

ROOT: The boss is waiting, Mister Batsumashball.

BOP: Batsumashball?

TAXI: Walk this way.

(*They start to walk.* DELORES *tries to tag along but* BOP *stops her.*)

BOP: Not you, Miss Au Lait.

(They fade as TAXI *and* ROOT *travel.)*

ROOT: Is it true what they say about Nauru?

TAXI: Every word.

(They arrive at The Ice Bucket. Lots of dry ice and neon tube gear.)

*(*SHRIMP *appears.)*

SHRIMP: Ah, our distinguished guest. Mister Batsumashball, I presume.

TAXI: Mister Shrimp, meet Mister Batsumashball.

SHRIMP: Mister Batsumashball. Delighted.

TAXI: Mister Shrimp Bucket. So nice to be here.

SHRIMP: Cool your cuticles, Root. If you go down to the laundry, I think you just might locate that missing— item. And be sure to give our little friend a nice big tip for his trouble.

ROOT: No prob. *(He exits.)*

TAXI: Ah, Mister Shrimp. It is my understanding there are—Brothers Bucket.

SHRIMP: *(Chuckles)* You're in for a treat. Allow me to introduce my distinguished brother. Doctor. Gut. Bucket.

(Ominous underscoring. The Huey Newton chair, which has been facing upstage, now swivels around. It is GUT. *He is dressed like Huey Newton in the famous photograph: black beret, black leather jacket and pants, black boots. He has a black glove on one hand, a spear in one hand and a machine gun in the other. Almost the spitting image of Huey—except that he's white and very overweight.)*

GUT: Welcome to our humble hotel, Mister Batsumashball. Where we pursue our studies in American iconography and contemporary mythology.

TAXI: Your work is well known.

GUT: I certainly hope not. That would be—unfortunate.

(GUT *and* SHRIMP *share an unpleasant laugh.*)

GUT: Perhaps we should proceed directly to the demonstration.

(SHRIMP *wheels out the Dream Device.*)

GUT: As you know, Mister Batsumashball, we have only to perfect our delivery system to begin global operations.

SHRIMP: After that, it's clear sealing.

GUT: That's right, Shrimp.

SHRIMP: You got it, Gut.

GUT: Your world-wide electronics empire should solve all our problems.

TAXI: It should, shouldn't it?

SHRIMP: With a nice piece of change for you, Mister Batsumashball.

GUT: This is the Dream Device, Mister Batsumashball. A dream recorder and projector. It records on these discs—

(SHRIMP *holds up a shiny disc and inserts it.*)

GUT: —and projects a holographic image. The apparatus is a complete package. It transcribes the dreamer's dream, records it, and plays it back. We got some help on this from Sony.

TAXI: You should have come to me.

GUT: We've been working with a guinea pig. Stealing and recording her dreams. An exotic dancer.

SHRIMP: Please Brother Gut. An ethnic dancer. She's a narcoleptic. She's a dreamboat of a dreamer. Wanna see one?

TAXI: I didn't come all the way from Nauru to pick pineapple out of my belly button.

(SHRIMP *flicks a switch on the Dream Device.*)

SHRIMP: You won't believe the fidelity on this. The three-D is stunning. This is her favorite. *If I Was A Fool To Dream.*

(DELORES *appears in a spot.*)

IF I WAS A FOOL TO DREAM

DELORES: I'm in a bar, sweetheart
Alone again, it's true
I'll have a scotch to start
A chaser for these blues

I'll have another shot
And wait for you to show
Someone will ask me out
I'll have to tell him no

I'm in a state, sweetheart
Alone, what else is new
I'll have a scotch to start
My memories of you

If I could have you back
I'd change my foolish ways
If I could kiss your face
I'd never ever stray

Oh my darling so I'd say
Never leave me never go
Always take my breath away

(*Spoken:*)

I've kissed a lot of guys
They've asked me to be true
I've told a lot of lies
'Cause none of them were you

I'm in a sorry state
My heart is sad and blue
When I turn out the light
I'll dream a dream of you

I was a fool to dream
I was a fool to dream
I was a fool to dream

(Spot on DELORES *out.)*

(Lights up on GUT, SHRIMP *and* TAXI.)

TAXI: She's so real.

SHRIMP: That hologram's patented. Our trademark: palpable image. Wait'll you grok the Clam Room Show. It'll knock your sox off.

GUT: Now, Mister Batsumashball. You're probably wondering why. Why collect dreams?

TAXI: It had double-crossed my mind.

GUT: Why not cash? Precious gemoids? Negotiable securities and other instruments of financial torture?

TAXI: Why not?

SHRIMP: Profit.

GUT: And power.

TAXI: How do you get profit and power from dreams? Mister and Mister Bucket, I still don't smell those greenback dollahs.

GUT: You have an extraordinary command of the American idiom, Mister Batsumashball.

SHRIMP: The aboveboard legal side of the market is enormous, Mister Batsumashball.

GUT: We'll be selling a modified version of this machine to psychoanalysts, therapists of every persuasion, and so on. And a home-use model—for the self-involved.

SHRIMP: Gonna be the biggest thing to ever hit Manhattan.

TAXI: You want me to perfect your long range dream stealer —

SHRIMP: You'll get a share of the net.

TAXI: Gross, there's no such thing as net.

SHRIMP: Oh, you're sharp, Mister B. Okay, gross.

TAXI: *(Snaps fingers)* Dream piracy. On a global scale. The legal stuff for therapy will be chump change if you can pry open anyone's head in the world and extract their dreams like a gherkin.

SHRIMP: Go for it, Mister B. Figure the angle.

TAXI: Gotta be cable. Mondo Video.

GUT & SHRIMP: Video Mondo!

TAXI: Thousands of new channels. They all need material. You tap into hot sources surreptitiously. Writers, artists, real DREAMERS. You suck out their dreams, like calamari, record 'em—and either screen the stuff raw, or put it into development.

SHRIMP: Now you're cooking with canned heat.

TAXI: Stealing dreams is much safer than stealing scripts.

SHRIMP: Hey, you can't copyright dreams.

GUT: Scripts for the insatiable maw of popular entertainment. The demand is endless, the supply anemic.

SHRIMP: And writers's block. You know how many writers out there got block? Many. Heads full of great plots and no way to get them out. It's like having a copper mine without a railroad.

GUT: We should capture all markets. Cable is just the beginning. Today, cable. Radio. Television. Hong

Kong. After Hong-Kong—Hollywood. It's the great big banal American dream, Mister Batsumashball: the conquest of Hollywood. The Heartbreak will replace Hollywood as the world-wide center of self delusion and primary source of pre-fabricated dreams. Brother Shrimp. If you please.

(SHRIMP *wheels in a portable deep freeze: rhinestones and neon trim. Clouds of dry ice.*)

GUT: I'm sure you've heard all the classic American myths.

SHRIMP: Every kid knows 'em.

GUT: About this or that legendary artifact.

SHRIMP: It's a government secret. Some old lady has Custer's scalp in a hat box.

TAXI: The saucer people who live in the top of Mount Shasta.

SHRIMP: Excellent, Mister Batsumashball.

GUT: That particular myth is indigenous to California. My personal favorite is the poodle in the microwave.

TAXI: They put the poodle in the microwave to dry it off. And it blew up.

SHRIMP: I heard it was a wet cat.

TAXI: What's your position on Bigfoot?

SHRIMP: Bigfoot's one of the best.

GUT: Do you ever wonder how these Native American myths germinate?

TAXI: Every day.

GUT: Metastisizing into myths of Bunyanesque proportions? For one simple reason, Mister Batsumashball—they're true.

TAXI: You got Bigfoot? I wanna see Bigfoot.

GUT: Perhaps this will convince you.

(SHRIMP *opens the deep freeze.*)

SHRIMP: We keep our extra extra special stock in here.
(He pulls out a hatbox, opens it and displays a mangy, moth-eaten blonde wig.)

TAXI: Custer?

SHRIMP: Who else?

TAXI: Your mother, maybe.

GUT: A hard sell, eh, Mister Batsumashball? Try this.

(From the deep-freeze SHRIMP *extracts and brandishes a thin metal cylinder, three-feet long and shaped like a cigar.)*

TAXI: *(With reverence)* Dillinger.

GUT: The one and only. According to popular mythology, Dillinger's—distinguishing anatomical peculiarity was detached after his demise and preserved. Pickled. In a jar.

SHRIMP: Smithsonian.

TAXI: I heard Walter Reed Hospital.

GUT: The value of this item only increases over the years as the stories grow more elaborate.

TAXI: Hard to exaggerate about something like that.

SHRIMP: One item that lives up to its billing.

GUT: And now, the piece de resistance. Mister Batsumashball, if you would be so kind.

(TAXI goes into the deep freeze.)

TAXI: Dillinger, I never bought. Jealous, I guess. But Bigfoot—I gotta hunch about Bigfoot. Oh, boy, Bigfoot!

(He looks down into the deep freeze. WHEN YOU WISH UPON A STAR plays under.)

TAXI: Uncle Walt.

(GUT *and* SHRIMP *chuckle nastily.*)

GUT: Isn't he gorgeous?

TAXI: He looks better than he did on his last season. Those stories started just after Uncle Walt—after Uncle Walt—after he—went away.

GUT: They said he was terminal, so he had himself freeze-dried while he was still alive.

SHRIMP: Good career move.

GUT: Cryogenically preserved in a state of icy grace. In a tube in a tower of Sleeping Beauty's castle. Ready to return to us the day a cure is found.

TAXI: To create new and better Magic Kingdoms! The Second Coming!

SHRIMP: One of our better heists. And not easy. That Tinkerbell was a bitch.

GUT: Our interest in dreams and icons led us inevitably to Uncle Walt. The greatest purveyor of myth the world has ever known. Uncle Walt—what a dreamer. Once we've found a cure for what ails Uncle Walt—

SHRIMP: We'll bring him back to dream for the Bucket Brothers on an exclusive basis. He'll dream it our way.

GUT: Tickle those ivories! Palpitate those eighty-eights!

(GUT *and* SHRIMP *sing NO MORE MAGIC KINGDOMS, anthem of incredible evil.*)

NO MORE MAGIC KINGDOMS

GUT: No more Fred MacMurray

SHRIMP: No more Peter Pan

GUT: No more Pluto furry

SHRIMP: No more Pollyann—

GUT: —a!

GUT & SHRIMP: No more Cinderella
No more haunted house
No more Tinkerbells

No more Mickey Mouse

No more Magic Kingdoms
Uncle Walt's passé
He'll dream it our way, yeah

GUT: No more boring nature flicks

SHRIMP: No more prime time swill

GUT: No more son of Flubber tricks

SHRIMP: No more Haley Mills

GUT & SHRIMP: No more Jiminy Cricket
No more Song of the South
Give me Wilson Pickett
Instead of Donald's mouth

SHRIMP: Quack!

GUT: Quack!

GUT & SHRIMP: Quack!

No more Magic Kingdoms
Uncle Walt's passe
He'll dream it our way, yeah!

SHRIMP: We'll flip off the lid of Uncle Walt's id
He'll french Sleeping Beauty *adieu*

GUT: They'll hump real fast then share a repast
Of Thumper and Bambi stew

SHRIMP:
We'll bring back Annette in her sweater you bet
To give us our afternoon thrill

GUT: If Daisy and Don can't get it on Snow White and
the Seven Dwarves will

GUT & SHRIMP: No more Magic Kingdoms
Bucket Brothers rule
We'll dream it our way yeah
Oh yeah

(Big finish)

TAXI: That's some plan.

SHRIMP: A class scam. Worth billions.

GUT: That's conservative. With Uncle Walt under
our thrall, the Bucket Brothers will rule the world of
popular entertainment.

SHRIMP: So, Mister B. Are you in, or are you in?

TAXI: Count me in. It may be repulsive, but it certainly
sounds profitable.

SHRIMP: Terrific, Mister B.

TAXI: I couldn't help but notice Uncle Walt's missing
one of his cute little white three-fingered gloves.

(Music sting)

SHRIMP: Lost in the laundry. So embarrassing. We
always try to have Uncle Walt freshly pressed for
visitors. Now, Mister Batsumashball, what about a
little ethnic dancing to celebrate our new partnership?
I'm sure the girls would be happy to oblige. Specialty
of the house.

TAXI: I'd like to see another sample.

(A little miffed, SHRIMP goes through a few discs.)

SHRIMP: Let's see. *I R S Chainsaw Massacre—The Slattern
of Soho*—that's one of mine. And look out, it is hot—
let's see, here's a dud, *The James Taxi Show*—

TAXI: That sounds good.

SHRIMP: No, it's a sit-com.

TAXI: I heard it was comedy suspense.

(GUT *and* SHRIMP *exchange glances.*)

GUT: Where did you hear that, Mister Batsumashball?

TAXI: Word on the street.

SHRIMP: Word travels fast to Nauru.

GUT: Word on the street. I am continually dazzled by your grasp of the American idiom, Mister Batsumashball. And come. Tell me. How is it you know so much about the Mount Shasta saucer people and Bigfoot?

TAXI: We keep in touch on Nauru. We have television.

(BLIND SAX *and* ROOT *enter.*)

ROOT: Taxi never showed. Boss.

SHRIMP: What a surprise. So you heard his dream was comedy-suspense, did you, Mister B?

TAXI: A real nail-biter. (*He is sweating. He pulls the three-fingered glove from his pocket, and mops his brow.*)

GUT: I doubt that your high opinion of your own dream is shared by a significant portion of the viewing audience, Mister Batsu-taxi.

(SHRIMP *pulls a gun.*)

SHRIMP: And unhand that glove.

(TAXI *takes off his dark glasses and turban, and hands* SHRIMP *the glove.*)

TAXI: (*In the V O*) I had huevos rancheros all over my mugshot. I'd meant to grill Shrimp like a souvlaki. Instead, I'd skewered myself seven ways till Sunday. I'd always wanted my own weekly series, but comedy suspense, not sit-com. What the hell, you can't sneeze at residuals.

SHRIMP: You're the only residual around here. You're a guy with no secrets, talk to yourself like that. Stay for dinner. Gracie's made extra.

TAXI: I'd like to, but I left the top down on my convertible.

(GUT *twists* TAXI's *nipple.*)

GUT: Manners, young man.

(SHRIMP *relieves* TAXI *of his gun, and hands it to* BLIND SAX *who points it at the audience.* SHRIMP *redirects him at* TAXI.)

TAXI: You really think he should have that?

SHRIMP: The N R A supports the constitutional right of blind people to bear arms.

(TAXI *glances into deep freeze.*)

TAXI: Hey! What goes on here? There's no life support system hardware. Nothing to keep him hibernation fresh.

(*The* BUCKET *brothers grow very grim.*)

TAXI: (*In the V O*) The look on their faces told me I'd hit the bull's eye. It also told me I should have bitten my lips off.

GUT: A unfortunate accident.

SHRIMP: The support systems were unintentionally destroyed during the heist.

TAXI: But that means now he's worth less than a frozen fish stick.

GUT: We trust you can keep our little secret.

TAXI: No lips are seals.

GUT: I will miss our repartee, Mister Taxi.

SHRIMP: It was extra extra special.

TAXI: I look forward to Uncle Walt's comeback.

(TAXI *moves for the exit.* ROOT *stops him.*)

SHRIMP: He'll make his before you make yours.

(ROOT *grabs him.*)

SHRIMP: You're such a fan of the maestro, perhaps you'd like to join him.

(ROOT *forces* TAXI *towards the freeze.* TAXI *elbows* ROOT *in stomach. The* BAND *plays action-suspense underscoring.* TAXI *and* SHRIMP *struggle for* SHRIMP's *gun. Big fight stuff. Finally,* SHRIMP *pistol-whips* TAXI *across the bridge of the nose.* TAXI *crumples to his knees. He passes a hand over his face and looks at the red stuff on his fingers.*)

TAXI: God. Real blood. I hate that.

(*Reggae bass line*)

TAXI: (*In the V O*) I was about to join Uncle Walt in the Deepest Freeze of all. My reggae headache was taking an encore. Days like this made me think I should have stayed in grad school. Then it hit me.

(*Flashback music.* SHRIMP *is caught in a blinding spot.*)

SHRIMP: Mitzi's in home appliances now. She's cool.

(*Music and spot out.* SHRIMP *reels, rubs his eyes.*)

SHRIMP: I haven't had a flashback like that since Tim Leary and I went barbecuing with Bobby. How do you do that?

TAXI: How do you do the underscoring?

SHRIMP: Trade secret.

TAXI: Flukey ditto.

SHRIMP: Enough shop talk. Hook him up.

(ROOT *pushes* TAXI *into the freezer and begins to attach him to some ominous looking machinery.*)

TAXI: Mitzi's gotta be in the ice bucket. But where?

SHRIMP: You're the detective.

TAXI: Yes, yes I am. Over there. The walk-in cooler. Home appliances.

SHRIMP: How terribly perspicacious of you, Mister Taxi.

(SHRIMP *opens a closet.* MITZI *in a tube, played by* DELORES *in a shower cap.*)

TAXI: Is she in the same shape Uncle Walt is?

GUT: Her pulse is glacial, but rock steady. As long as we defrost properly, she'll be good as new.

(SHRIMP *closes door on* MITZI.)

TAXI: (*In the V O*) It was all beginning to fall into place, like pecs and mams on a fortieth birthday. Mitzi on ice. The Bucket brothers' hologram fooled me, and I was ringside.

SHRIMP: I'm dying to hear the rest of this, but too much denoument always gives me gas. Which reminds me— (*To* ROOT) Turn on the liquid nitro. *A bientot*, Mister Taxi.

GUT: *Bon soir*, Mister Batsumashball.

(ROOT *turns on the liquid nitro. It makes an evil hiss.* GUT *and* SHRIMP *cackle madly.* TAXI *starts to quiver and shake and turn blue. The* BAND *plays suspense music.* DELORES *bursts in, armed with a Dirty Harry-sized Magnum, followed by* LIZZY *and* SALLY, *who are also armed with smaller pistols.*)

DELORES: Hands up, Buckets. (*To* ROOT) Nix the toxic waste, Rootie-tunes.

(ROOT *turns off the nitro.* GUT *points spear and machine-gun at* DELORES. SHRIMP *aims* BLIND SAX *at the* BALKANETTES.)

GUT: Likewise, Miss Con Leche, let me urge you to do the same.

SALLY: Shrimp, your ass is file gumbo now.

SHRIMP: Is this what they call a Mexican standoff?

DELORES: I think I'm gonna ventilate you.

SHRIMP: A tough-talking woman with a Magnum always turns me on.

DELORES: You are one sick Shrimp, you know that?

SHRIMP: Since you put it that way—let me put it this way. And this way. And what about this way?

(As SHRIMP *puts it various ways, the* BAND *plays some exciting kung fu fighting music and* ROOT *whirls and twirls and disarms* DELORES. LIZZY *and* SALLY *in a series of astonishing lightning moves.)*

DELORES: Oh! You! You! You Buckets, you!

SHRIMP: I promised you kung fu fighting. In you go. Join your flat- footed friend.

*(*ROOT *puts* DELORES *in the deep freeze with* TAXI.*)*

DELORES: Sorry, Tax.

TAXI: I fell for it, too.

SHRIMP: Balkanettes, too. You don't want to dance ethnic, I'll find somebody who does.

SALLY: Shrimp salad, I hope you deep-fat fry in fast-food hell for this.

SHRIMP: And after all I've done for you.

SALLY: Bite mine!

*(*ROOT *stuffs the* BALKANETTES *in the freezer.* DELORES *looks down.)*

DELORES: Who's that?

TAXI: Uncle Walt.

DELORES: My God.

TAXI: Mine too. *(To* SHRIMP*)* Let me put this other glove on him, will you? He looks naked without it.

(SHRIMP *tosses the glove to* TAXI, *who puts it on Uncle Walt.*)

DELORES: You dream-sucking Buckets! Why are you putting the snatch on my dreams? Why are you making me dance in my sleep?

TAXI: Allow me.

(*Music*)

SHRIMP: Go ahead, Tax. I just love it when you detect.

TAXI: The whole enchilada?

SHRIMP: Be incisive. Relentless. We'll just wither.

TAXI: Everybody ready?

BAND:: Hit it, Tax!

TAXI: Okay. But if I leave anything out, don't stop me—
cause—

(*The* BAND *segues into DOIN' THE DENOUMENT.*)

TAXI: I'm doin' the denoument
Red herring, McGuffin, crazy cat's paw
I'm doing the denoument
I'm runnin the whole thing down

ALL: Denoue
Denoue
Denouement

TAXI: The Buckets invent the Dream Device
They put the snatch on poor Uncle Walt
Stash his technicolor ass on ice
Plan his final comeback from their secret vault

GUT & SHRIMP:
We wanted to cure him not waste him
You gotta believe it's not our fault
We only meant to gently baste him
With crocodile tears and cryogenic salt

TAXI: *(Spoken)* Tell it to the judge

GIRLS: Shrimp is kinky for ethnic dancers
They hired Mitzi and sucked her dreams

TAXI: Doped to the gills with Gut's enhancers
She somnambulated into their evil schemes

ALL: He's doin' the denouement
Red herring, McGuffin, crazy cat's paw
He's doin' the denoument

TAXI: I'm runnin' the whole thing down

ALL: Denoue
Denoue
Denouement

TAXI: They wear Mitzi out she starts to get wise
To keep her from blowin' the whistle
Put her tutus and tango shoes on ice
That's the preamble now here's the epistle
(Spoken—to audience)
You try to rhyme whistle—it's not that easy.

SALLY: Thistle!

SHRIMP: That's the meat, now here's the gristle?

TAXI: Oh, please. *(Sings)*
Con Leche comes lookin' for Mitzi

SHRIMP: We advertised for another thrush

DELORES: You couldn't call the Clam Room ritzy

GUT: We slipped her a pill in her Chardonnay blush

ALL: He's doin the denoument
Red herring, McGuffin, crazy cat's paw
He's doin' the denoument

TAXI: I'm runnin' the whole thing down

(The BAND *vamps.)*

TAXI: If you don't mind, I'll do the rest in prose. Rhymed exposition is murder.

SHRIMP: Put a Perry Mason on it, Tax, and let's wrap this tuna in nori—

TAXI: I always get suspicious when I see a stiff being carried into a fleabag hotel. In this case, it was a frozen stiff. Uncle Walt.

GUT: We'd sent him out to a specialist. But there was nothing to be done.

TAXI: The three-fingered glove belonged to Uncle Walt.

SHRIMP: That camembaert Professor Alors dropped it. I'll settle his hash later.

TAXI: No, he didn't. By the way, Professor Alors and Doctor Gut—

(Ominous underscoring)

TAXI: —are one and the same person.

(All gasp.)

SHRIMP: Don't be ridiculous.

GUT: You're hallucinating.

TAXI: *(To others)* Ever seen them in the same room at the same time? Think about it.

SHRIMP: It's a theory.

TAXI: Once I figured out you were stealing Con Leche's dreams, I intercepted Mister Batsumashball to find out why. And now I know.

GUT: Everybody wants to be in show business.

(The BAND surges up.)

TAXI: *(Spoken)* That's it! *(Sings)*
I'm doin' the denouement
Red herring, McGuffin, crazy cat's paw

I'm doin' the denouement
I'm runnin' the whole thing down

ALL: Denoue
Denoue
Denouement

SHRIMP: Now that's private detection!

(Big finish)

GUT: Where is Mister Batsumashball?

TAXI: Stashed in the breakfast nook off the lobby.

SHRIMP: Sheer clam nectar, Tax. Hey, we're having some fun now. Okay! Enough denouement! Let's ice these turkeys! Liquid nitro and lots of it!

(ROOT turns on the liquid nitro. Dry ice billows. THE BOP OP bursts through the door, wearing a tatty Blackglama mink. He has a gun and he flashes a badge.)

BOP: Special Agent—Lillian Hellman! You're now on ice, Buckets. *(To audience)* The first time I met Dashiell Hammet, he arrested me for shoplifting costume jewelry at Lamston's. He was a Pinkerton, I was a Pulitzer Prize winner. We laughed about it later — the little fox.

TAXI: *(In the V O)* Meanwhile, in another part of the forest, The Bop Op was undercover, stringing the Buckets along like a couple of sausages.

DELORES: When did you know the Bop Op was a cop?

TAXI: Just now, when he flashed his badge.

BOP: Drop 'em, Buckets.

(ROOT unties everyone, while SHRIMP and GUT drop 'em. BOP turns BLIND SAX and points him at the BUCKETS.)

BOP: Special Agent Lillian Hellman. Investigating the theft of Uncle Walt from Sleeping Beauty's castle. Your name is mud, Buckets. What else is in there with Uncle Walt?

TAXI: This.

(TAXI *hands* BOP *the cylinder,* BOP *gets awe-struck and sensual.*)

BOP: Dillinger. Do you know how long the Bureau's been after this? (*Takes it from* TAXI *and hefts it*) What becomes a legend most.

TAXI: I suspected you might be on our side.

BOP: Special Agent Lillian Hellman. FBI and Copyright office.

SHRIMP: Hey! You can't copyright dreams, I'm telling you.

BOP: When did you start to catch on?

TAXI: From jumpstreet, pal. You dropped the three-fingered glove. Not to mention the passkey and putting my piece back in my pocket.

SHRIMP: Mink turncoat.

BOP: And who says private dicks are slow?

TAXI: I want my wallet and watch back, brown belle.

(TAXI *gives him claim check.* BOP *gives* TAXI *his wallet and watch.*)

DELORES: Sure is complex.

TAXI: If you're experiencing narrative motion sickness, don't let it get you down. It comes with the territory. By the time we close the covers on this one, you won't remember which ends are loose.

(TAXI *takes a sad look at the thawing Uncle Walt.*)

TAXI: He's starting to melt. How could you?

SHRIMP: We didn't mean to break him.

GUT: Obviously. His resale value in this condition is nil.

SHRIMP: We even had to refreeze.

TAXI: *(Aghast)* You're never supposed to refreeze. *(Near tears)* Poor Uncle Walt. No comeback now. Entertainment as we know it will never be the same.

GUT: No more Magic Kingdoms, Mister Taxi.

TAXI: Lillian!

BOP: Yeah, Nancy?

TAXI: Put these perverts where the sun don't shine!

BOP: You got it.

(He starts to herd off GUT, ROOT, SHRIMP, and ZOOT.)

TAXI: You don't look very worried.

SHRIMP: *(Laughs)* Me? We have more lawyers than the District of Columbia. I'm about as worried as Standard Oil at tax time.

TAXI: Don't plagiarize my style, Bucket.

SHRIMP: Hey! You can't copyright style, I'm telling you.

GUT: We'll meet again, Mister Taxi. In the sequel.

SALLY: Come catch our new act, Mister Taxi.

TAXI: Wouldn't miss it.

(LIZZY and SALLY exit, singing NUEVO HUEVO.)

TAXI: Thanks for your help, Lillian.

BOP: My pleasure, Nancy. Call me. We'll have lunch. *(Laughs girlishly)* We'll leave you two flamingos alone.

(Everyone exits.)

DELORES: Taxi! What about Mitzi?

TAXI: We'll come back for her tomorrow. One more night—she'll never know the difference.

DELORES: Taxi, she's my kid sister.

TAXI: I know. And believe me—where I come from, that counts for something.

DELORES: Listen, there are still a lot of things I don't understand.

TAXI: Don't sweat it. The genre teaches us to accept the inexplicable. It's a very metaphysical genre.

DELORES: If you say so. Listen, Taxi. Thanks. No, seriously.

TAXI: All in a night's work.

DELORES: I guess I've seen the last of you.

TAXI: In a pig's valise, sister.

DELORES: I never thought you'd work that in.

TAXI: It came to me in a dream.

DELORES: I like your style.

TAXI: Likewise, in spades.

DELORES: May I call you Nancy James?

TAXI: I wish you would.

DELORES: *Besame mucho!*

(DELORES *grabs* TAXI *and kisses him hard, bending him over in a tango swoon. In the middle of the kiss, he breaks off.*)

TAXI: *(In the V O)* She had lips as sweet and full as ten pounds of sucre in a five pound sack. They turned my spine to flan. I was diving head- first into a pool of passion-fruit punch, hoping I'd never have to come up for air.

(DELORES *drops* TAXI *on the floor.*)

DELORES: You gotta see somebody about that. I'm not spending the weekend with somebody who talks to himself in the past tense.

TAXI: Promise.

(TAXI *picks himself up.* DELORES *and* TAXI *lock eyes and get steamy.*)

DELORES: I don't care what they say about you. I think you're muy picante.

TAXI: What exactly do they say about me?

DELORES: That you're fast as a claims settlement.

TAXI: Irony. I like that in a woman. You know, Con Leche, you're about as subtle as a pitcher of sangria.

DELORES: Tell me more, big fella.

TAXI: You come on strong, like you're a double shot of tequila with a brew back. But you're really about as tough as a spring day.

DELORES: Sweet. You hard-boiled guys have maple sugar in your veins.

TAXI: Don't stop now.

DELORES: Taxi, you come on like a mouthful of razor blades, but you're really as hard-edged as a flour tortilla. You're as sweet as sopapilla.

TAXI: I've swapped similes with saps from Sunset to Sepulveda, but sister, you're something special.

(*Music*)

TAXI: I like a gal who can spin a phrase.

DELORES: I like a guy who can torture all day a figure of speech.

TAXI: Not to mention syntax.

(DELORES *and* TAXI *sing (If I Was)* A FOOL TO DREAM reprise.)

DELORES & TAXI:
I've been alone so long
It doesn't matter why

Others have come and gone
I kissed them all goodbye

Cause they weren't you, my dear
Until you came my way
I spent my nights alone
And dreamed away my days

I've been alone so long
I couldn't speculate
If I would recognize
You as my lucky day

I'm in a state, sweetheart
Of transcendental grace
I'll skip the scotch, instead
I'll kiss your silly face

If I was a fool to dream
Ah true love would come my way
Darling let me dream and never wake

Got a ballad to spare
It's bittersweet but true
Got a love I can share
A serenade for two

I've been a fool too long
It doesn't matter why
I'll be a fool for you
And kiss my blues goodbye

(*Sweet finish*)

DELORES: You're like a day at the beach, big fella.

TAXI: Baby, by me that's okay.

(DELORES *and* TAXI *lock eyes, get steamy, etc.*)

TAXI: Chaka chaka chaka cha.

(*A sizzling kiss*)

DELORES: Let's blow this clam bar.

TAXI: Which way out of Dodge?

DELORES: Scrape the gum off your shoes and walk this way. *(She starts off.)*

TAXI: Not a chance. Wait. I have something for you.

*(*TAXI *pulls the cylinder out of the deep freeze.* DELORES *takes it from him.)*

DELORES: Dillinger.

TAXI: It ain't Bigfoot.

*(*DELORES *sizes them both up.)*

DELORES: I may need this. Let's go find out. Undulate, Tax! Undulate! *(She undulates off.)*

TAXI: *(In the V O)* It was time to give my faithful amanuensis "Legs" Lichtenstein a ring. Time to tell her to hold my calls, take in the mail, and put out the cat. Let's face it, it was time to undulate. I advise you to go home and do likewise. *(Beat)* I wonder where you buy those little white three-fingered gloves?

(End credits music up.)

*(*DELORES *and company come back and sing a reprise of* NEVER JUDGE A THRILLER.*)*

DELORES & GIRLS:
I'm a thriller babe
A serenade
A killer babe
I'm so glad you came
You skimmed my pages sweetheart
And followed my plot
You found all the good parts
Cause I'm Hot Hot Hot

COMPANY:
Never Judge a Thriller by its cover, NO
Never Judge a Thriller by its cover, NO

I'm a best seller babe

Read me straight through

We'll give away the ending

And make this old prose new

Never Judge a Thriller by its cover NO
Never Judge a Thriller by its cover NO
Never Judge a Thriller by its cover NO

Never, Never, Never, Never, Never
Never, Never, Nooo

Never, Never, Never, Never, Never
Never, Never, Nooo

(Repeat as needed)

(Big finish)

END OF PLAY